GuitarPlayer

PRESENTS

GUITAR HEROES
OF THE '70s

Guitar Player

PRESENTS

GUITAR HEROES
OF THE '70s

EDITED BY
**MICHAEL
MOLENDA**

**Backbeat
Books**

AN IMPRINT OF HAL LEONARD CORPORATION

Portions of this book are adapted from articles that originally appeared in *Guitar Player* magazine, 1970–1984.

Published in cooperation with Music Player Network, New Bay Media, LLC, and *Guitar Player* magazine. *Guitar Player* magazine is a registered trademark of New Bay Media, LLC.

Published in 2011 by Backbeat Books
An Imprint of Hal Leonard Corporation
7777 West Bluemound Road
Milwaukee, WI 53213

Trade Book Division Editorial Offices
32 Plymouth Street, Montclair, NJ 07042

All text content courtesy of *Guitar Player* magazine/New Bay Media except articles by Steven Rosen, used by permission.

Printed in the United States of America

Book design by Damien Castaneda

Library of Congress Cataloging-in-Publication Data

Guitar heroes of the '70s / edited by Michael Molenda.
     p. cm.
 Title appears on item as: Guitar player presents guitar heroes of the '70s
 ISBN 978-1-61713-002-1
 1. Rock musicians–Interviews. 2. Guitarists–Interviews. 3. Rock music–1971-1980–History and criticism. I. Molenda, Michael, 1956- II. Guitar player. III. Title: Guitar player presents guitar heroes of the '70s. IV. Title: Guitar heroes of the seventies.
 ML3534.G86 2011
 787.87092'2–dc22
 [B]
                              2010045187

www.backbeatbooks.com

Contents

Foreword

BY STEVE LUKATHER

WHEN I GOT THE CALL TO WRITE THE FOREWORD TO this book, I was more than blown away, as I am a fan of the great guitarists of this era. As an admirer and fellow player, the '70s were my true coming-of-age decade. In the early '70s, I was still reeling from the Beatles' life-changing effect on me, as well as that of the Stones, all of the great pop music and players of the 1960s, and the explosion of Jimi Hendrix, Jeff Beck, Eric Clapton, Jimmy Page, and . . .

Well, I am not going to list everyone else, because then this will become *my* book, and I am not worthy of that. However, the impact of the '60s music revolution had absolutely carried over to 1970 and all the years that followed. It was ON!

The guitar players you will read about in this book took what the old blues players did to yet another level. I would be hard-pressed to explain what each player in this book did to help define '70s guitar in some way, because I believe their work speaks for itself. But I do want to make clear that the '70s was a time of not copying anyone. It was a time of really pushing to find your own sound and voice—and that is exactly what each of these players here have done.

I know I personally spent days, hours, and years lifting the needle off my record player (kids: Google the term to find out what this thing was) over and over and over again—even slowing records down to 16 RPM to try and figure out solos and guitar parts note for note. Now *that* was ear training and a test in patience. I thought my parents were gonna kill me after I played the same part of a tune 100 times, devouring all I could in trying to get what these guys were doing.

And, remember, this "self-education process" was often made tougher because no one sounded the same—*ever*. That was the point. We would go to concerts early in order to see the gear, and wonder how these players got the sounds. Then we'd be blown away by the organic sounds and natural ability we could only aspire to. This decade brought us some of the finest players to ever pick up the instrument, as well as sounds and solos and songs that are timeless.

Again, as they are all so different, it is so very hard for me to break these players down. In many cases, they are not only people I grew up listening to and learning from but also friends of mine. Also, musicians get very different things out of the same influences—which is *how* they forge their own style and become instantly recognizable from the pack. Even if they played the blues, they still had a totally unique sound. That was the quest. And it was much harder back then, because you could not get to these mystical people who created otherworldly sounds, and then, as the decade moved on . . . *chops!*

The nice thing was that time seemed to move slower. Life had a slower pace. It wasn't the fast-food mentality that currently exists. Please understand that I am not putting down what is happening today, as there *are* genius players now. I'm simply saying that it was harder to get there because, back then, there was no prior standard, and everyone was pushing the envelope all the time. For example, simple three-chord rock evolved to dense music with odd time signatures, to wild, atonal fusion chops, to experimental long-form compositions, to permutations of classical-blues-country-jazz and what would become metal. There were no digital samples or multi-effects boxes or computers to get "that" sound.

In fact, about the only real way to find out *how* anyone did what they did—or got the sounds they got—was through the first real guitar magazine: *Guitar Player*. We all read *GP* cover to cover because it was our only real source. This was where the players talked about their amps, their guitars, the few stomp boxes that existed, and their customized rigs. Those sounds seemed to come from aliens, and were almost unattainable. It was humbling, but if you knew how to play like any of these guys—or knew their solos—you were elevated to a higher place amongst your peers. And that place was *deserved*, because, let's face it, it was really hard to hear some of the intricacies of what was on those vinyl gems—let alone *learn* what was on them . . . correctly!

I still listen in awe of these masters; and, like a fine wine, all these players have grown, and kept their music and styles alive. I am honored to have grown up and started my own career in the '70s, and to have made friends with some of my heroes in this book. In some cases, I even got to play with them. I am very blessed and lucky.

I hope you enjoy what is in this book. I know I do, and there is always something to learn—a lick you missed on all these classic artists' records. The world "timeless" comes to mind once again because there is a reason these guitar players are so important and have stood the test of time. Take the time to check them all out; you will be better for it.

November 2010

Guitar Player

PRESENTS

GUITAR HEROES
OF THE '70s

Randy Bachman takin'
care of business.
(COURTESY OF *GUITAR
PLAYER* MAGAZINE)

BY STEVE ROSEN

JULY 1975

Randy Bachman

HAD RANDY BACHMAN NEVER EVEN PICKED up a guitar, his talents as a songwriter and producer would have been enough to implant his name firmly in the Canadian music hall of fame. With Guess Who pianist and vocalist Burton Cummings, Randy co-wrote "These Eyes," "Undun," "American Woman," "Laughing," and many others. He has since gone on to produce all of Bachman-Turner Overdrive's albums, and even played a large part in the production of Brave Belt (his band immediately following the Guess Who). But now, he is being hailed as a guitarist worth his weight in fancy riffs, and he's even come to be called "The Legend" (as has his custom-built Stratocaster).

In fact, during the days when Keith Emerson was with Nice, the group's arranger liked Bachman's guitaring enough to ask him to come to England to play with Emerson, who was forming a new group. Bachman's solo album, Axe, with touches of classical, country, rock, and flamenco styles, indicated his eclectic capabilities, but a gallbladder infection necessitated a long hospitalization, which ended his chances of strumming even one chord with the group that became known as Emerson, Lake and Palmer.

The violin was Randy Bachman's

first contact with music, and he remembers those early days as unhappy. It was a "very terrifying" time in his life.

"The violin turned into a sore spot in my life," he recalls. "When I was 10, 11, and 12, all my friends were going out to play football or going to the movies, while I was up in my room practicing violin. And when I was bad, instead of saying, 'Go to your room—you can't have dinner,' my parents would say, 'Go to your room and practice your violin.' This thing that was supposed to be a pleasure, they made a punishment."

Numbed by his experience with the violin, he stayed away from music for over three years, until age 15, when he saw Elvis Presley on Tommy Dorsey's television show. Presley, dressed in black shirt and white tie, so dumbfounded Randy that he was moved to ask, "What's that around his neck?" Somebody said, "It's a guitar." Bachman was so intrigued by all the excitement beamed at this performer and this "thing" around his neck, that he instantly had to try his hand at guitar. His cousin owned a large acoustic Martin, and, after being shown three fundamental chords, Randy was picking out songs. When his mother told him there was a guitar in the attic he could use, he found that it was, in fact, an old Hawaiian Dobro with painted palm trees on the body and a large nut to raise the strings. Soon the nut was removed (to lower the action), the strings were replaced, and within two weeks of learning his first three chords, Randy could outplay his cousin.

One guitarist who had a great influence on Randy was Lenny Breau. Lenny—who was at that time working with his parents' travelling country-rock show—introduced Bachman to fingerstyle picking, as well as to the genius of Chet Atkins.

"I waited around until after the show, and I asked Lenny what was he doing," says Bachman. "He said, 'It's called Chet Atkins style,' and I thought he meant 'chetatkins'—a one-word title, like 'flamenco.'"

From watching Lenny perform with the Hal Lone Pine Caravan, Randy was able to master the Chet Atkins fingerpicking style, and, because of Atkins's sojourns into jazz and flamenco, the still-young guitarist developed a liking for the lighter jazz and classical pieces.

"I'd play hooky from school to go watch Lenny practice," Randy says. "He lived right across the street from my girlfriend, and after watching him figure out a piece, I'd run back over to her house and try it out myself. Meanwhile, I spent two years in every grade, but that didn't mean anything to me."

This Canadian-born guitarist, with these assimilations of styles, went on to form the Guess Who, Brave Belt, and, most recently, BTO. He admits to being highly influenced by the English sound—especially the early heyday of British rock, when the Who and Jimi Hendrix started making their presence known.

"The Guess Who were pretty much just getting started," he recalls, "when I saw the Who at the Marquee Club. They played so loud I thought somebody had fired a gun in my ear. To see all this destruction was utterly phenomenal. When we got back, we started doing stuff like "My Generation," and smashed up our stuff. We'd make fake speaker bottoms, and I'd take a guitar and throw it about six or eight feet across the room, and it would stick into my speakers. Along the way, I developed some nutty ideas on my own about how to make my guitar sound like I wanted it to—and how to make my amplifiers sound the way I wanted them to—and I've come up with certain little gimmicks that I use on my own."

Bachman's first electric guitar was a black Silvertone guitar which cost $79, and was (according to Randy) one of the first electric guitars in his hometown of Winnipeg. No one told him he also needed a guitar amplifier, but Randy figured there must be some way to hear his guitar, so he had friends make jacks so that he could plug it into television sets and tape recorders. After blowing out numerous family TV sets, he was forced to purchase an authentic amplifier. His first was a Harmony, which was replaced shortly thereafter by a Silvertone sporting two 12" speakers and a reverb unit.

Randy has since gone on to purchase about three dozen instruments. For quite some time, his main guitar has been the Fender Stratocaster—though this instrument is altered almost to the point of non-recognition. This is the instrument dubbed "The Legend," and even Bachman says, "You'd have to see it to believe it."

A 1953 model, this Strat's original neck was somehow ruined and replaced with a slightly wider and rounder rosewood Jazzmaster neck. Still not satisfied with it, Randy removed the neck and bridge pickups and in their place put a humbucker and a Telecaster pickup, respectively. Then, he took out the three-position pickup selector, and substituted three on/off pots. He can now achieve any combination of the Legend's three pickups.

"I do all this wiring myself," Bachman points out. "I don't know what I'm doing—it's all trial and error. I end up getting a lot of solder burns and a lot of shocks, but the sounds I can get out of this guitar are amazing."

The Fender tuners have been substituted alternately with Grovers and Schallers, and Randy has even changed the standard nut (or "frog" as he calls it). Usually made of bone or plastic, several nuts have split due to Bachman's choice of heavy bass strings to provide a strong bottom for chording. From high to low, he uses Ernie Ball strings, gauged .009, .011, .013, .040, .050, .060. Because of their thickness, the lower strings tended to sit on top of their nut grooves, and Randy was forced to file the grooves periodically to insure proper seating. He eliminated this nuisance by removing the troublesome nut, and then gluing one of his mother's metal knitting needles in its place. Originally, he did not cut any notches in the needle, opting to let the strings float freely over the round metal surface. Since then, he noticed the nuts slipped around a bit more than he desired, and he filed grooves into the metal for all the strings except the G and B. The vibrato arm on the Legend has been removed because it constantly caused the guitar to detune.

Because of his obvious interest in altering guitars to achieve the right sound, he realizes, as well, the importance of the proper amplification. After much experimenting, he has found that two, 200-watt Sunn Model-T heads powering Marshall and Heil speaker stacks are an excellent vehicle. One Marshall cabinet is loaded with four 12" Celestions, the other is loaded with four 12" Altecs, and the two custom-built Heil cabs contain 12" Heil speakers.

Randy uses a heavy triangular pick, although he does do a great deal of fingerpicking. He once tried using fin-

"DY-NO-MITE" DISCS!

Bachman-Turner Overdrive, Bachman-Turner Overdrive, 1973

Bachman-Turner Overdrive II, Bachman-Turner Overdrive, 1973

Not Fragile, Bachman-Turner Overdrive, 1974

gerpicks, but discarded them because it annoyed him to have to keep putting them on and taking them off.

Randy uses few exterior gimmicks, though he does use a Fuzz Face, a Vox wah-wah, and, occasionally, a Leslie speaker (on record only). He believes in being a "straightforward-sounding guitar player," and only uses pedals when he feels they will actually be creative.

Randy has concrete ideas about which direction his playing will take, but candidly admits he feels that what an artist wants, and what an audience wants, are often two different things.

"Unfortunately, your public picks what they want from you in this business," he says. "And if you don't do it, you're crazy, because you want to make a living. For example, I started doing a country thing with Brave Belt, and the public quickly told us what they wanted by not buying it. So now I try to do what the public wants, and, at the same time, try to please myself. Hopefully, I'll get a turn to do what I want later."

Jeff Beck working his whammy-bar magic. (COURTESY OF *GUITAR PLAYER* MAGAZINE)

BY LOWELL CAUFFIELD

NOVEMBER 1975

Jeff Beck

JEFF BECK IS NOT READY TO LET HIS GUITAR playing rest on its own laurels. He has already made weighty contributions with a legendary stint in the Yardbirds in the '60s, as well as later endeavors in various groups he has formed. Those heralded accomplishments, however, are only so much history. Beck, now in his early 30s, has gone through what one of his associates appropriately called a "musical rebirth."

After a lark with Tim Bogert and Carmine Appice in 1973, the British guitarist retreated to a reclusive life style at his home in rural England. This year, he re-emerged on the music scene with an album entitled *Blow by Blow*. A guitar-dominated disc, it shot to the top of the sales charts in a matter of weeks—quite a feat for an all-instrumental album. But beyond its high listenability, the album displayed new directions for Beck, who has moved into a mode some call "jazz-rock." Beck's unmistakable style remains, but jazz leads and more involved rhythms and chording also grace his latest vinyl effort.

With the album's success, Beck and a new band (Max Middleton on keyboards, Bernard Purdie on drums, and Wilbur Bascomb on bass) made a tour of the United States on a double bill with another musical innovator,

John McLaughlin and his Mahavishnu Orchestra. In Detroit, Beck agreed to talk about the increasingly popular jazz-rock fusion, and the movement of his guitar playing towards that style. Relaxing in his dressing room, he was friendly and attentive, although, earlier, he had given three encores—one where McLaughlin had joined him for a jam—and had a second, sold-out concert to do later the same evening.

Did you move towards jazz for the sake of expression, or because it was more of a technical challenge?

Both. It really wasn't too much of a challenge, because if anything gets the better of me, I leave it. But it was nice to hear myself play something else than basic rock.

> 66 Rock is an energy to me. It's more complex now than it was, but it's rock just the same. 99

Were there any particular records that led you in that direction?

I'm not a record freak. If I get a tape, I'll play it in the car while I'm driving someplace. But I don't sit down and religiously listen to records. I just buy a handful of tapes that knock me out—things like Billy Cobham, Stanley Clarke, and all the great rock and rollers. I call Billy Cobham a "rock and roller" because he's so forceful. Rock is an energy to me. It's more complex now than it was, but it's rock just the same.

But the licks you are playing, they are nothing like the clichés on your 1968 album *Truth*.

No, No. That's gone. It's finished. Everybody has been doing them—like Humble Pie, you know. Mick Ronson tries to do it. Jimmy Page does it still, and he gets away with it—he makes a living at it.

Do you think audiences—especially the older ones—are getting sick of most rock sounds?

They're not getting sick of it, but they need to be led some other place. They need to be given the opportunity to get into some other things. I suppose I could get a group and go out there and clean up by singing about rot, and playing "I Ain't Superstitious" by turning it into nostalgia. But *that* is nothing new. I'd rather have people start shouting with "Cause We've Ended as Lovers"—something that has some class. Because it's written by Stevie Wonder, that gives it immediate class.

From the technical end, have you been listening to one musician in particular that influenced your guitar playing?

Yes. I listened to Jan Hammer—the Moog player from the previous Mahavishnu Orchestra. He also played with Billy Cobham on *Spectrum*. That gave me a new, exciting look into the future. He plays the Moog a lot like a guitar, and his sounds went straight into me. So I started playing like him. I mean, I didn't sound like him, but his phrases influenced me immensely.

Do you play a lot of scales?

No. I play the notes I think I want to hear. I don't practice a scale. That's very hard—very depressing. In fact, it's exactly the opposite: I like to play easy things that *sound* hard.

On *Blow by Blow* though, in some cuts you run up the neck in rapid-fire, notes–jazz style. Were you capable of doing that, let's say, five years ago?

Oh yeah. But it was so out of place in the music I was doing then. I would sound like I was showing off all the time. When you have an intricate rhythm section, it fits in.

Does it help to learn how to read music?

It doesn't help me at all. After all, nobody is following the little dots. The audience isn't going to clap because you've hit every little dot. They're going to clap because they like what they hear. That's the way I look at it—it's far away from the standard set of rules laid down by the concert pianists. If they don't play their pieces absolutely by the book, they boo you off. You know, even if they miss the last note in the concert [*laughs*]. That's too heavy for me.

You're still improvising a lot, then?

Oh, yeah—just jazzing around. There's no sense restricting yourself in music. It's supposed to be there to give you freedom.

Have you been jamming with anyone during the layoff you've had since Beck, Bogert & Appice?

I don't jam. I'm a country boy, and there are always things to do with the house, garden, cars. When I'm finished doing what I have to do, I play to relax. I don't get up at breakfast time and practice.

You're not a six-hour-a-day man, then ?

No. I think that's a good way to be great, but then you fizzle out—you peak too soon. I want to peak out just before I die, you know [*laughs*].

Has playing with Max Middleton, who's quite jazz-influenced in his keyboard work, helped your musical growth?

Very true. When I want to put something into practice, I always call Max up, because he can get the right piano, and play just what I have in mind. His backing is so fantastic that it makes a simple lick sound great. He encourages me in everything I want to do. He's incredibly enthusiastic.

Did he draw you out?

He draws out something in me that I've been afraid would be there which is, like, *taste*.

Nothing wrong with that.

No, but it could put me out of a job, you know [*laughs*].

On the song "Diamond Dust," there's orchestration. Are there any difficulties working with strings?

I hated it when I first heard it, because I was so used to listening to the track without it. Like you go into the studio fresh the next morning, and you think, "Ahh, that's a nice track. Leave it alone." Then you overdub, and you hear people messing around with the mix, and you get used to it, and then when you finally hear the strings on it you think, "Oh, my God!" But it's too easy to kick the stuff off. You have to live with it awhile. I take my recordings home and listen to them so that I know I'm giving them a fair chance. If, after a month or so, if I hate what I've done, I take it off.

Have you made any equipment changes?

I'm still using the same wattage output—200 watts with two Fender speaker cabinets and two Marshall tops. I have the amp miked, though. I used to use Sunn amps. The Marshall tops give you the right sort of gritty sound. The Sunn is a bit too clean. The Fender speakers are a bit more

"DY-NO-MITE" DISCS!

Rough and Ready, 1971

Blow by Blow, 1975

Wired, 1976

reliable than the Marshall speakers, but the Marshall top is better, I think.

You used your 1954 Les Paul Standard on the album and tour, but also some Stratocasters. I thought you had given up on Stratocasters?

No. I don't know. It's just a good stage guitar, although it's technically a bitch to get a hold of and play. But it comes over well, and it slices through the atmosphere with the highs.

What accessories are you using?

An overdrive booster and a wah-wah. The boost is just a preamp—it's not a fuzz box—that gives you instant power, sustain, and distortion.

What is the principle behind that bag and tube you use that makes your guitar sound like it's talking?

It's a signal from the guitar that comes up the tube. When I hit the note, it will come up the tube into my mouth. Then, you can "play" the sound into your mouth through the tube, and make the sound do what you want just by moving your mouth. That was invented about 40 years ago in "Sparky's Magic Wand"—a kid's record they used to play. This kid used to go for piano lessons, and he had a dream where his piano came to life, and started talking to him. It was a voice by a piano chord going "Spaaaarky." It was great, and that's where the idea came from.

If you could make a generalization, what would you call the music you're making now?

It crosses the gap between white rock and Mahavishnu, or jazz-rock. It bridges a lot of gaps. It's more digestible—the rhythms are easier to understand than Mahavishnu's—but it's still on the fringe.

There are many guitarists who are in rock and roll ruts. What advice would you have to get out of that—to help someone expand into different musical veins?

That would make it too easy for them if I told you, wouldn't it? I've spent half my life trying to get out of ruts. You've just got to do what you do best. Get a band you really like playing with, and just go. If you're in a depression, it's a personal thing. Pull yourself out of the personal depression, and start playing. If everything is jumping around you, you jump with it. The music usually reflects what's going on in your personal life.

Ritchie Blackmore showing his
Stratocaster some tough love.
(FIN COSTELLO/REDFERNS)

Ritchie Blackmore

RITCHIE BLACKMORE, LEAD GUITARIST AND CO-FOUNDER
of Deep Purple, was born in Weston-super-Mare, England.
Emerging to fame in America in 1968, with the hit single "Hush,"
Deep Purple has appeared with the Royal Philharmonic at London's

BY MARTIN K. WEBB

JULY/AUGUST 1973

Royal Albert Hall, faced 4,000 rioting fans in Stuttgart, and been smuggled out of a concert hall in Iceland in a paddy wagon. Blackmore's first guitar was a secondhand Spanish type, which he has since replaced with Stratocasters and Gibsons. Recently, his solos have been pushed forward in Deep Purple's overall sound, which has been recorded in the normal studio setting, as well as less orthodox places—such as when their album, *Machine Head*, was made in a hotel corridor in Montreux, Switzerland.

How long have you been playing guitar? Did you ever have lessons?

I've been playing for about 14 years, and I had classical lessons for a year. That helped, because I learned how to use my little finger. A lot of blues guitarists play with only three fingers, so they can't figure out certain runs that require the use of their little fingers. Classical training is good for that.

Has classical training affected your playing in any other way?

I would say it shows up most in the music I write. For example, the chord progression in the "Highway Star" solo—*B minor, D♭, C, G*—is a Bach progression. The classical influence is always

there somewhat, but I don't intentionally use it that much. I play a lot of single notes, and that's not classical.

How do you rate Steve Howe, as far as putting almost strict classical stylings into a rock context?

He's very good at it, but he's not the kind of guitarist I can listen to. He's very good at runs, but I don't like that type of playing much.

When you were first starting out, were you influenced by anyone in particular?

At that time, everybody else was copying Hank Marvin and the Shadows. In the beginning, Duane Eddy used to be my favorite. I also got into James Burton and Scotty Moore, and Big Jim Sullivan was a big influence. He plays with Tom Jones now. He's very good, but he's kind of wasted with Tom Jones. Big Jim used to live practically next door to me. He had only been playing about two years, but he was just about the best guitarist in England, straight away. I thought I was learning pretty well, until I saw him. I couldn't even understand what he was doing. So I used to sit on his doorstep, and when he'd come out, I'd ask if I could come in. He taught me quite a lot of tricks. I think he used to get a bit fed up with me hanging around. But when you're around someone that good, your own standards are raised. It saves you a lot of trial and error.

Did you ever do much session work?

Yes—when I was about 17. Some of the work was a drag, but some of it was interesting. Session work makes you more strict, because you can't hit notes all over the place. You've got to make each note really count. When you're recording, if you're not really clean in your playing, it sounds like a mess. You may think you sound fabulous on stage, but when you hear yourself played back on record, it's just disastrous most of the time. If you can play well in the studio, you can play well on stage.

Do you modify your Stratocasters?

Not much. I screw the middle pickup all the way down, because otherwise it gets in the way of the pick. I really only use the neck and bridge pickups. It wouldn't do me any good trying the special "in-between" positions on the pickup selector because I'd be knocking the switch out of position constantly.

You prefer the sound of Strats, right?

Yes—because they have a more "attack-y" sound.

What is the main difference between playing a Strat and playing a Gibson?

A Stratocaster is harder to play than a Gibson. I don't know why. I think it's because you can't race across a Strat's fretboard so fast. With a Gibson you tend to run away with yourself. It's so easy to zoom up and down the neck that you end up just playing scales or chord shapes, rather than really working for an original sound. Overall, playing a Fender is an art in itself, because they're always going out of tune. But I've got it pretty well under control, because I actually play very lightly.

How loud do you crank up your amp?

Full up! I've always played every amp I've ever had full up, because rock and roll is supposed to be played loud. Also, keeping the amp turned up is how you get your sustain. I turn down the volume on the guitar for dynamics. I've also had my amps boosted. I know Jim Marshall personally, and he boosted them for me so that they're putting out about 500 watts. The people at Marshall said they're the loudest amps they've ever heard. I had an extra gain stage built onto it, and a couple of more valves. That's why things just tend to disintegrate every two weeks. I blow out speakers all the time. I only use one of my two stacks. The other is just a spare in case I blow up the other one.

Does that happen often?

Sometimes, I have a run of bad luck where something blows up every gig. You feel like giving it all up when that happens. Learning to play the guitar is one thing, but learning to play with a big amplifier is a different thing altogether. It's like trying to control an elephant.

But you can't get that power rumble without big amps.

Yes, but that's about all. I'd rather play a little amp anytime. I used to do the circuit with a little amp, and I played ten times better than I do now. I was fast and clean, but nobody took any notice except other musicians. Normal people didn't know what the hell I was doing.

What's that thing on the drum case behind your amplifier?

It's a Hornby-Skewes treble booster that's modified with a variable control to let me dial in more or less sustain. With a Stratocaster, I don't really need any treble boost, so I use the unit mostly for sustain.

You don't use any other effects?

I don't use pedals—wahs and fuzzes and whatnot. I used to, but I found I couldn't get a good, natural sound with them. Even when a wah-wah pedal is turned off, the sound is very thin. You'd always find that with Hendrix, for instance. So I just use my fingers for different sounds and effects.

When playing live do you stick closely to your recorded solos?

I try. Unfortunately, the only one I can remember is "Highway Star." I can never remember what I do in the studio.

What sorts of things can affect the quality of your performance?

Some nights, I feel like I can do anything. Other nights, I feel inhibited. It all depends on what I'm feeling. If I go on stage and think, "That guy in the front row thinks I'm an idiot and that I can't play the guitar," I'll seize up. But if just one person says, "You're great," I really get turned on to play. If I overhear someone saying something like, "This guy is useless—I'm not staying to watch," it doesn't do me a hell of a lot of good.

When do you feel you play best?

Actually, I can play best if we're having a jam session. The stuff we do on stage is always basically the same, so I like to jam now and then to keep in shape. The best I ever played this year was around Christmas at a jam in Hamburg, Germany, with some of my old friends. I thought I played brilliantly, because I wasn't leaping around. I was just standing there with small amps.

You don't like leaping around on stage?

I like leaping around on stage as long as it's done with class—like Free. They're the best band in England. Paul Rodgers is a good singer and a brilliant mover. None of this jumping up in the air and doing the splits and all that. He just moves with the music—not like Pete Townshend who has gotten to the point where he waits until the photographers are aiming at him before he leaps. He's not very spontaneous.

Do you believe Townshend was the first to use feedback?

Pete Townshend was definitely the first. But not being that good a guitarist, he used

"DY-NO-MITE" DISCS!

Machine Head, **Deep Purple,** 1972

Made in Japan, **Deep Purple,** 1973

Burn, **Deep Purple,** 1974

to just sort of crash chords and let the guitar feedback. He didn't get into twiddling with the dials on the amplifier until much later. He's overrated in England, but, at the same time, you find a lot of people like Beck and Hendrix getting credit for things he started. Townshend was the first to break his guitar, and he was the first to do a lot of things. He's very good at his chord scene, too.

You've said Jeff Beck is one of your favorite guitarists. What is it about his playing that you find inspirational.

Jeff Beck is so great to listen to because he takes chances, and when it comes off it's very emotional. When he gets feedback going right, it's like an orchestra playing, instead of just a guitar with a lot of brilliant runs. Actually, the real art of chance music is knowing what to do if you don't get what you tried for. It's like when a ballet dancer falls over—they have to know how to get out of looking clumsy. Beck takes a chance every night. Sometimes, he's absolutely useless, and you wonder why he has a name. Other times, he pulls things off that sound like nothing you've ever heard before.

What advice would you give to a person who wanted to become a good rock guitarist?

I'd have a tendency to say, "Get a good guitar and a good tutor book." But, really, the only way you can get good—unless you're a genius—is to copy. You'll never come up with your own sound until you've copied someone else's. That's the best thing—just steal.

Mike Bloomfield honed his blues prowess by hanging out at Chicago clubs as a youth. (PHOTOFEST)

BY MICHAEL BROOKS

JUNE 1971

Michael Bloomfield

DRIVING NORTH ON CALIFORNIA'S HIGHWAY 101, thoughts of what Michael Bloomfield—the once-controversial blues guitarist from the Paul Butterfield Band, Electric Flag, and Supersession experience—would be like brought on unlimited speculation. A few minutes after crossing San Francisco's Golden Gate Bridge, I turned off the freeway on an exit marked Mill Valley, leading to a small, secluded community which moves to the beat of the nearby metropolitan area. Waiting only minutes in front of his humble Mill Valley home, I spotted a curly-haired young man walking down the sidewalk with a friend at each side. After a brief greeting, we went inside and the interview began.

When and where was the first time you picked up a guitar?

I started playing guitar when I was 13 years old, and I had a guitar teacher for about a year and a half. He taught me chords and theory—what little I know—and also some lead and stuff. Mostly, I would just learn chords and play rhythm to famous standards while he played lead.

What kind of music were you into then?

I was into '50s rock and roll—the AM radio type. Carl Perkins, Sun Records music, Chuck Berry, and whatever was on the dial. But I'd prefer "Rumble" by Link Wray to maybe something by Duane Eddy, just because it was funkier. I always lean toward the funkier sound. Very rarely would I hear blues or black music.

But when I was around 14 years old in Chicago, way at the end of the radio dial was a show called *Jam with Sam* that played stone blues, man. I just liked that music most of all. I even went down with a friend of mine to hear Muddy Waters. We took a bus, a train, and then another train to the club—two little kids going down there to a funky bar. They wouldn't let us in, so we just stood outside and listened.

At the same time, I was really interested in folk music, but real commercial folk music like Odetta, Bob Gibson, and Josh White. As I got older, I got real interested in more ethnic-type folk music. I call it ethnic music, but if it were like blues, I would prefer Lightnin' Hopkins to Brownie McGee, because he seemed more real. Now, it's all mixed together, but then it was polarized into definite categories.

What about your guitar playing?

I was just a regular hot-licks kid. I wanted to learn. Like, if you wanted to play in a rock and roll band at that time, you had to be the guy who could play just like Duane Eddy, Buddy Holly, Chuck Berry, the Virtues, or the Ventures, or anything like that. It was the guy who could copy every guitar solo exactly from the record note for note—just perfect. So that's what I tried to do. At the same time, though, I was hearing that stuff on the blues radio stations, and I was trying to throw as much of that stuff into my playing as I could. By the time I was 15, I was a real fast, bluesy, rock-and-roll guitar player. I had all the notes, but I wasn't putting them in the right places at all. It took many years later for that to develop. I mean, it took me a long time to get interested in singing—not me singing, but listening to vocal sounds. The finest guitarists are those who can imitate voices. The more vocally you can play guitar, the more human you're going to sound.

Where did you go from the blues-rock thing?

I stopped playing electric and started playing acoustic. I got me a Martin, and I started learning folk music. I was really interested in playing ethnic folk music, bluegrass, and Travis picking. By the time I was 18, I was about as good at that as anyone in the world has ever been. I mean, I was a mean picker at that time.

What about the Paul Butterfield thing?

I was playing on the north side with a blues band, and Paul was with an all-black blues band on the south side. He got a really good band together, and when they hit, they were like dynamite. It was the best band I had ever seen at that time. Then, a guy from Elektra Records asked Paul if he wanted to make an album, and Paul asked me if I wanted to play a little slide for him. I admired Paul incredibly for his singing and his music, but I never liked him, so I was kind of reluctant to do it. Finally, I agreed, and I played piano on a few tracks because Elvin Bishop was their guitar player. But I did play slide on two or three numbers.

What did you use for your slide?

I used a bicycle handlebar—cut off to about an inch. I find that sounds the best. Anyway, after that thing, Dylan called me.

Did you know him?

Yeah. He had played in this club in Chicago, and I had heard his first album, and I thought it was shit. I told him that, and he said, "I'm not a guitar player, man, I'm a poet." So we sat and talked and played all day, and we got to be friends. Then, he left, and I didn't see him until he called me up, and asked if I would play on a record with him. Now, I had no idea he was famous at this time—that he was sort of a superstar. I learned "Like a Rollin' Stone" and a few other songs, and then we cut that album—*Highway 61* or whatever it's called—and, later, we played at Newport. By this time, Paul saw me playing guitar in a go-go club, and he decided he wanted me in his band. I told him I was not going to play piano—that if he wanted me in his band, I'd have to play lead guitar.

How did that work out, then?

Well, at first, the Butterfield band was very idiomatic. We played just stone blues about as pure as you can play it. I think we passed the color line. We played that blues good, man. There wasn't a blues player we learned from—like Muddy Waters and those cats—who didn't say to us, "You boys are going to carry it on for us." Well, except for the singing, maybe. Muddy would tell Paul, "You're not man enough to sing it yet."

We were pretty young back then, but we did have the emotional feeling or nuance of blues music. There are so many nuances. For example, it's the kind of music in which you respond to it as it happens—not when it's done. That's Western European music culture—you clap when the music is finished. But in the black culture, you scream, you holler, you approbate, you say, "Yes! Wow! It's happening!" And this correspondence, this closeness with the audience, and this feedback was really necessary. You'll find this same thing with hillbilly music. If you hear a real good bluegrass show, the audience will start screaming as soon as the band starts a song.

But I don't get any response from performance today. It's just a bunch of stoned kids lying on the floor. They can appreciate all they want, but they're not from an oral tradition. They may scream when they hear a wild note, but they probably learned that from listening to one of B. B. King's live albums.

So you do still enjoy performing live?

I am very reluctant to gig live. I don't dig gigging live. It's not a question of intellectually digging it or not—I just don't react to it well. I get real nervous, and real uncomfortable, and I never feel that it's really worth it—other than to make the bread.

Then you dropped the Butterfield band, and then split out West and did the Electric Flag.

You know, for a long time, all of us in Paul's band had wanted horns. Many of our blues records—other than the Chicago stuff, and stuff that came out of the South and Detroit—had horns. And as a guitar player, I really wanted to hear that sound of the guitar interacting with horns. So when I went out to form the Flag, man. I wanted a good old blues band with horns in it. And all these diverse influences came into the Flag. By that time, I was into all kinds of music—the Beatles and other things on the radio. There wasn't any music on AM or FM that wasn't entering my head at one time or another, and leaving some sort of imprint on my mind. So if you want to really hear the Flag's playing in different bags, get *The Trip* album, because we tried to play every American musical style we could think of. We played everything—old jazz, Dixieland.

Were you satisfied with the Flag?

Well, the Flag was a good band, but it got incredibly pushed into the real-fast-to-make-it-real-big syndrome. We never had time to mature as a band, or even as people. The thing that made us close together was our obligation—we had to make this, we had to make that. We were really good a lot of times when we performed live, but a lot of times, well, we just had troubles. Buddy [Miles, Electric Flag drummer] was success-crazy. He was absolutely insane to make as much money as he could as fast as he could, and he would spend incredibly exorbitant amounts of money and buy giant cars. And we had some junkies in the band. There were just horribly diverse factions that can break up any band. And, most of all, I found myself being a stone product. If I had just a little more control, it wouldn't have been so bad. I don't mind being the product if I can also be the manufacturer. If somebody had taken control of the group, we would be together now. We'd have been even more beautiful.

How did that *Super Session* album with Al Kooper and Steve Stills come about?

I didn't want to make that record too much. It was just a favor for Al Kooper. He said we'll make a lot of bread out of it, and he was absolutely right. It made a million. I had just finished with the Flag, and I was really depressed. I didn't want to play any gigs at all. All I wanted to do was sit around and read. I have insomnia, and I told Kooper that, and said I probably won't be able to cut this record. He said, "Well, come on down and give it a try." So I flew to Los Angeles, and cut for him all day, and he rented this big fancy house with a swimming pool and everything. But I couldn't go to sleep, man—I was so uptight. So I snuck out early in the wee hours of the morning with a guitar in my hand. I got a cab and flew home. And when Al went to look for me in the morning, I was already back in San Francisco. So he hired Stills to replace me for that day. That's how it went. Stills is playing the wah-wah, and I'm playing the straight guitar—that's how you can tell who is who.

You play mostly by ear?

All by ear. It was like this door opened up to me, and I could play so much more by ear—so much more than just blues. I could play any mode or any framework. And being a fast guitar player really helps a lot. I've heard tapes of some Butterfield live gigs, where I've played so fast I just couldn't believe it. Now I'm really fast, but not like Alvin Lee. Not that kind of fast, but fast like Johnny Smith or Joe Pass— smooth and accurate. So I have these two musical concepts going in my mind: the purest blues, and this sort of un-pure, anything-goes-as-long-as-it's- harmonically-germane-and- harmonically-intelligent style of guitar playing. I'm working hard on both of them.

"DY-NO-MITE" DISCS!

Live at the Old Waldorf, 1976

If You Love Those Blues, Play 'Em as You Please, 1976

Analine, 1977

Lenny Breau masterfully fused many styles into his playing. (JON SIEVERT/GETTY IMAGES)

BY MARTIN K. WEBB

SEPTEMBER 1974

Lenny Breau

JAZZ GUITARIST LENNY BREAU, THE SON OF country and western singers Lone Pine and Betty Coty, has been described by Chet Atkins as "the most exciting new guitarist since Johnny Smith. I predict he's going to turn out to be the number-one guitar player."

Johnny Smith had warm words of his own for Breau calling him a musician who "has created a new concept and direction for the electric guitar."

Breau's guitaring style has evolved in complexity so that the young, now Canadian-based artist, has come to rely on all five fingers of his right hand for his intricate, simultaneous comping and melodic explorations. His first attempts on the instrument came when he was seven; Lenny became as a polished enough guitarist at 12 to move with his parents onto the country-music trail leading out of Wheeling, West Virginia. It was appropriate that Chet Atkins—his first and perhaps greatest influence—also helped Breau get into his first recording studio. Chet heard the then unknown guitarist in Winnipeg, Canada; encouraged him to send a demo tape to RCA; signed him to a recording contract; and helped produce his first album, *Guitar Sounds from Lenny Breau*, which was followed by *The Velvet Touch of Lenny Breau—Live!* The latter album

had been recorded before an audience at Shelly's Manne-Hole in Hollywood during one of Breau's infrequent trips to the United States.

When did you first get involved with jazz guitar?

I guess by the time I was about 17 or 18, I got my first gig doing jazz. I had always dug jazz, right from about the age of 12 years onward, but I was sort of out of context with it.

Who was influencing you?

When I first started digging jazz, I listened to a lot of Barney Kessel, Tal Farlow, Johnny Smith, and, of course, Chet Atkins. He's not a jazz guitarist, but he's still the first guitar player I ever heard who really did something to my head. I got my fingers going with the Chet Atkins style of guitar playing. After that, I sort of started studying music. I was using the same approach, but with a jazz style in mind. I feel I owe a lot to Chet Atkins in terms of how I play the guitar, because he opened up a lot of doors to me. Another main influence is jazz piano. After about eight years of listening to jazz guitar players, I started listening to jazz piano players very seriously. And in that area, one of my main influences is Bill Evans. There's something about piano players. They're better schooled or something. Like, usually, a piano player can do the whole thing—playing the harmonic structure of the chords, as well as the melody. You can learn a lot from listening to piano players, because it seems that they are more evolved in musical knowledge, whereas a lot of guitar players who have played in the country bag, or in other bags, haven't even bothered.

> ❝ After a while, if you're a mature musician, you just play what you play and try to be honest. ❞

Do you fit into that category?

Right. I never had any formal training. I never went to a school or anything. I learned most of what I know right on the bandstand through firsthand experience, and through getting together with other musicians and asking questions. The guitar is a folk instrument, and it's the one that most people can adapt to. You can carry it around with you and all that.

Is it true that your playing style evolved after you listened to Les Paul records without knowing they were overdubbed, and you learned how to play them anyway?

I've heard that, but it's not true. At first, when I listened to Atkins, I thought that there was some trick involved, but then I realized there wasn't. As far as overdubbing was concerned, I always knew what it was. I admire Les Paul very much as a guitarist and musician. I dig what he has done. He was into that sound trip years ago, getting sounds way back then that I haven't heard anyone reproduce since.

What do you think has distinguished the jazz guitarist from the rock guitarist?

It seems that with the rock player, the main thing is the blues, or the rhythm and blues scale—which is used a lot with maybe one or two others. Now in jazz guitar, you're using a lot of scales, and I think that that's the main difference. Jazz players are using a lot of different colorings and chords and stuff. It's not a folk music. It's not so down-to-earth. But that's all changing now. After the Beatles came out, rock started to become more sophisticated, so I can't say that rock musicians are tied down so much by the blues scale anymore. I'm just speaking in generalities when I say that. I'm just saying that when I hear rock, I seem to hear a lot of blues—which I don't hear when I listen to jazz.

Do you think jazz players are becoming more open to using rock and blues techniques such as string bending?

Oh yes, I can see a lot of that beginning to happen. John McLaughlin, I would say, has got to be the number-one rock player and jazz player when it comes to performing new music with rock in it. He has it all down. The Eastern thing is there also. John is a great guitar player.

Hasn't Larry Coryell successfully combined the two styles?

Yeah, but he doesn't really play the same style. They're two different cats. Polls and that sort of thing are just silly, because it's not like a boxing match. After a while, if you're a mature musician, you just play what you play and try to be honest. I mean, when you look at something like the *Playboy* All-Star Jazz Band, and see cats like Jimi Hendrix, Henry Mancini, and Johnny Cash all in the same band, you know just where the whole poll thing is at.

How would you account for the increasing difficulty to get record dates playing straight jazz?

The guitar is the main instrument of rock, and I think that has put a damper on jazz guitar. I know a lot of jazz guitarists who have sort of laid back for the last eight, nine, or ten years, and haven't recorded like they used to. I mean, let's face it. The people who run the business are in it for the money, and they aren't going to record something that won't sell in huge amounts. You almost have to be a guitar player to go out and buy a jazz-guitar album. The run-of-the-mill person isn't going to go out and buy a jazz-guitar album by a specific cat, because that isn't the kind of thing they're playing on the radio. You almost have to be a special kind of person to know what you want, and how to go about getting a specific album. You almost have to be a musician.

Are you saying that jazz guitar music might be too subtle for the average listener?

It demands listening. A lot of people just want to dance, and you can't dance to most of it. Of course, that depends on how you dance. There is actually a lot of jazz guitar still being recorded today, but it has a rock beat and a rock coloring. Like the overall sound may be disguised to the point of sounding like rock, but what they are really playing is jazz. It just seems that the main thing is to not mention it's jazz—*then* you can sell the album. So a lot of cats are using that approach. They're just playing what they want to play, and not sticking a label on it.

How did you come to use a solidbody Hagstrom 12-string with only six strings?

I had the 12-string around for a while, and I was going to use it as a 12-string, but something happened to my 6-string one day just before a gig, and I needed another one fast. So I decided to see what would happen if I took six strings off the 12-string, and used it like that. I discovered that I liked it better than an ordinary guitar, because it gave me more room to work in, and made it easier to play chords and stuff in the higher octaves.

Isn't your choice of a solidbody different from many jazz guitarists?

I used to use Gibson hollowbodies a lot. I loved them, but I like a ringing sound. I liked the sound that a lot of rock and blues players were getting, and I noticed that most of them were using solidbodies, so I began to use them, too. I like the bass strings to ring, and on some of these nice old hollowbodies, I was finding that the bass string would die away too fast. Like you'd play a chord, and the top strings would ring on, but the bass would just sort of die. So I just started grabbing any kind of guitar that would ring the way that I wanted it to without caring what it looked like, or what it was. I use the bass a lot in my technique, and there doesn't really seem to be any safe way of choosing a guitar nowadays, because as soon as a company becomes well-known, the quality of their work seems to go down. Most large guitar companies have a peak period somewhere between the point where they first become competent, and the point where they start to get too many orders.

What kind of amp are you using?

GBX. I was working with Anne Murray for a while, and they laid all these amps on the band, and I started using it, and I liked it. The amp isn't as important to me right now as the guitar, though, because I want to get something different. The kind of guitar I really want can only be custom made, because what I want is a doubleneck. I want a 7-string guitar on the bottom, and a 14-string guitar on the top. It would be just like a 6- and 12-string doubleneck, only it would have double and triple strings on the bass ends. Not an extra playing string like George Van Eps's or something. I'm having a hard time trying to find somebody who will do this for me, though. A lot of big companies are not interested in making a custom guitar, because they've got a lot of money tied up in what they're selling right now, and they just don't have the time to do it. At least that's the only reason that I can think of.

But when I get the guitar that I want, I want to tryout a whole bunch of amps and try and get the right one. I don't really know enough about them to talk about them. All I know is when they sound right. I don't know enough about electronics to explain what I want, but I'd like to sit down with an electrician sometime, and do it back and forth.

Do you use any special setting on the one that you're using now?

I don't have any particular one. I try and get a sound that's not all highs. I try and

"DY-NO-MITE" DISCS!

Five O'Clock Bells, 1977

Mo' Breau, 1977

The Living Room Tapes, Vol. 2, 1978

get a full sound, and you've got to use a certain amount of bass to do that. So I do that, and then mix the treble over that.

What about your thumbpick and nails?

My thumbpick, and the way that I use it, is just like Atkins's. I take care of my nails pretty much the same as any classical-guitar player would. I guess I would have to say that you have to treat them as part of your instrument and part of your sound. They're as important as anything else. I've had to get used to using my left hand when it comes to lifting something up. And you learn certain things by experience—like to open doors with your left hand, so that if somebody is coming in on the other side, you won't break a nail.

Fingerpicks are a lot less trouble, and they're used a lot in folk playing, but in jazz playing I wouldn't want to use anything but my nails. I think fingerpicks are kind of clumsy. Most people who use them are people that would wear down their nails faster than they would grow back. But I use fairly light strings for a jazz player: medium D'Angelicos. The only other guy I know who uses fingers in jazz is Van Eps. But all I'm really doing is using almost classical-style fingerpicking—except for the thumbpick—and I'm approaching the guitar in a musical sense as if it were a piano.

Did Chet Atkins also influence you in your use of harmonics?

Yes, I learned that from him, and like everything else, I just adapted it to jazz. I feel that it gives the guitar a whole different sound—a whole different shading. And when you go back to the normal sound, it changes again. So what I'm trying to do is get all the different kinds of colors, shades, and ranges out of it that I can.

Roy Buchanan—
one of the true
masters of the
Fender
Telecaster.
(COURTESY OF
GUITAR PLAYER
MAGAZINE)

BY ROBERT BERMAN

MARCH 1972

Roy Buchanan

SO WHO'S ROY BUCHANAN? HE'S A 31-YEAR-OLD legend. For five or six years he has been working with Danny Denver and the Soundmasters in a tiny bar a couple of miles outside Washington, DC in Bladensburg, Maryland. Not too many months ago, you could call him the finest unknown guitarist in the world. Many people did. But now, with articles in a few newspapers and a TV special about him, you'd have to call him the finest semi-known guitarist in the world. Then again, you might be among the growing numbers of people who simply call him the finest guitarist in the world.

Among his admirers are Eric Clapton, the Rolling Stones, Merle Haggard, Johnny Otis, Robbie Robertson, Hank Snow, Henry Vestine, Al Kooper, Kim Simmons, Mundell Lowe, and Nils Lofgren. And among his fans are thousands of people who have faithfully made the pilgrimage to the Crossroads, where Roy usually plays for all the stompers and late-'50s boppers. And now, there are the millions who were turned on to Buchanan by Bill Graham and the National Educational Television Network last fall.

As a father of five, Roy has hesitated about going out on the road—even turning down the Rolling Stones. And, then again, he has been

Guitar PLAYER

Annual Artist Issue

CHET ATKINS
JAMES BURTON
JERRY BYRD
ROY BUCHANAN
LEO KOTTKE
OSCAR GHIGLIA
CAROL KAYE
JESSE FULLER

around quite a while, has paid his musical and drug dues, and can't see himself scuffling to be a rock and roll star.

The following interview was done by Bob Berman—a true Buchanan freak who wrote us offering $1,000 to any reader or staff member who could show him a better guitarist. Now that's faith.

Where were you born and raised?

I was born in Arkansas, but when I was about two, we moved to Pixley, California. I left to go on the road when I was about 14, and have been traveling ever since. In California, I just went to school and worked in the fields once in a while.

When did you first develop an interest in music?

I actually started listening to music when I was about five years old. My father always liked it—he used to listen to the radio and things. I told him one time that I liked music, and he said, "What do you like best?" I said, "guitar." That was when I was five or six. He bought me one right after that, and I started picking it up myself. Then it broke, so I didn't get another one until I was nine or ten. That's when I really became interested in it.

Why the guitar?

It sounded like a versatile instrument, and I've always liked different types of music. I wouldn't want to play a horn, because I couldn't get the chords and other things on it. One of my first inspirations was a guitarist named Roy Nichols. He was raised around Bakersfield, California. I used to catch him on television and radio. He's with Merle Haggard now. And I listened to all the regular cats like Chet Atkins, Hank Garland, and Grady Martin. Today, though, my favorite is Barney Kessel. Kessel for jazz, Jimmy Noland for blues. And B. B. King—everybody likes him. But Barney, because he always played it straight. He didn't have to have any gimmicks. He played what he felt, rather than having a flash thing.

You studied music at the beginning, right?

Yeah. I studied steel guitar for three or four years, but I gave it up because I wasn't really interested in anything other than the regular guitar. I studied it for my folks—they wanted me to learn it. But I never learned how to read music. And I haven't practiced in ten years [*laughs*]. Playing with other people is even better than practicing—it's experience. My first group was a trio when I was about nine. We played a little bar for about six months. Since then, I've, worked with quite a number of groups. I was with Bobby Gregg who had a hit called "The

Jailman" about 1962 or '63. I played with Dale Hawkins, too. He did "Suzy Q." I worked with Ronnie Hawkins. The first thing I ever recorded was "My Babe" with Dale. I did a couple of things with Freddie Cannon, but I can't remember the names.

They're still playing your lick on "Suzy Q" today. Did you make a lot of money back then?

Oh, yeah. I got rich [*laughs*]. I made about $100 a week, and all I could drink.

Do you feel bitter about the past—about working so hard for so little money?

No. I mark everything up as experience. You learn not to do things that way again.

What has kept up your interest over all these years?

I always wanted to play what I felt, but when working with other people, it has to be kind of commercial. Even when they let me do what I wanted, they held me back to a certain point. I couldn't go all the way, because they were inter-

> " Like, to me, fuzz tone is only distortion, so I used to slice my speakers with razor blades, and soak them in water. "

ested in selling—in making all that money with a Top Ten record. But now it seems like anything sells, and you have more freedom. You can play jazz, and the kids seem to be buying it. Blues—it's whatever you want to play.

Is it true you turned down an offer to work with the Rolling Stones?

Yes. That came about through my first manager, Charlie Daniels. I never actually met the Rolling Stones, but they had heard of me some way or another. They mentioned to Charlie that they wanted me to tour with them. The main reason I decided not to go with them—beside the fact that I don't want to travel—was that I didn't know the material, and I didn't figure I could do the job right. To sit down and learn all those songs—that would have taken a lot of work. I guess I'm lazy. I figured that there were other people who knew the music better.

There are a lot of rumors—particularly in Europe—about you. You and James Burton are the main ones people in Europe ask for. Have you ever thought of going over?

Well, most of them know that I don't like to travel. I like to stay in my own area. The only way I would think about traveling would be for myself—if I had a hit or something on my own.

When did you first meet James Burton?

It was at the Skyway Club in Shreveport, Louisiana, about 1957 or '58. They tore it down since then. It was Dale Hawkins's group. All the musicians would come down on Friday nights and jam. I came down once in a while, and that's how we met. I thought he was good—really commercial. He knew how to make a hit, which he did, as far as I'm concerned. We played together on stage three or four times. We lived together for about a month in LA in 1959. We never worked together in the same group, though. We'd just go around once in a while and sit in with other groups.

Why did you leave California?

I got a job in Las Vegas, and I lived there for about a year. I was young, so I wanted to travel.

Are the musicians today better than when you started playing?

I wouldn't say better. They've had a lot more people to listen to. I guess you would say they're improving faster. Rock and roll is always going to be here, but the competition is getting tough. You're going to have to be a little bit better.

Where is the music scene going from here?

I think that jazz and blues and rock will be kind of combined together. The players will have to get better and more versatile.

Let's talk equipment for a while. What type of guitar do you use?

A Stella [*laughs*]. No, I've got a Fender Telecaster—a 1953. I like it, because it's the funkiest. And it's versatile. You can play jazz . . . I think it's the best all-around guitar. It's not modified—I just keep it stock. I use Fender Rock and Roll strings.

How often do you change them?

When they break.

Don't they lose their sound before that?

Probably.

Do you prefer the one-piece maple neck to the rosewood model?

It was the grain in the wood that I think I liked. The feel of it makes it better. It's harder for me to bend a note on a rosewood neck. Maple is easier to work with. And I like the action high, because it keeps your technique built up, for one thing. You won't get lazy if you have to work a little harder. I have a tendency to get slouchy with the strings too low, and they get like a "popping" sound, and they rattle. Notes sustain better when the action is high, too.

When you sustain, do you use hand vibrato or just finger action?

A little of both, but I keep my thumb around the neck for strength and balance.

And do you bend the notes by pushing the strings or pulling them?

I push them up.

When you fingerpick notes while playing with a pick, how many fingers do you use?

Sometimes, only one or two. Sometimes, all of them. It depends on the feel of the thing. I think my technique came from playing steel when I was young. You have to play steel with fingerpicks. You can play with a flatpick, but it limits you. I used to use fingerpicks on the Telecaster, but now I just use fingernails. The flatpick I use is a little Fender jazz pick. It's like a mandolin pick or something—very small and heavy. Big picks get in my way. The smaller the pick, the better I can get around.

Do you pick in any unconventional style?

Everything I do is unorthodox. I hold my pick wrong. I use my thumb, which you're never supposed to do. When I'm picking blues, though, I'll do a lot of downstrokes. When I want speed, I use a small circle.

You've perfected an overtone technique by striking the string with your pick and the first finger at the same time. Did you develop this yourself?

I guess so. I never heard of anybody else doing it, and I've been doing it ever since I can remember. When I first did it, it was a mistake. I did a thing with Bobby Gregg called "Potato Peelings," and it happened. Then, everybody was digging that one thing, so I just figured out what I did.

When you do it in blues, you move down in every position, and basically do it on the high notes to get the effect of bringing the note up then dropping it down, say a full step. Then, you'll ring the note. It's very effective for blues, but do you use it in other material?

It'd be hard to use it in jazz, because you have to have a lot of volume, and you have to have the guitar on treble. But when I play jazz, I usually have a lot of bass. On some country things I'll use it, though.

You can produce a pedal-steel effect with and without manipulating the volume knob on your Telecaster. Which method do you prefer?

I really don't prefer one over the other. You use the palm of your right hand kind of as a mute when you hit it, and the volume sound comes up. I don't know how to explain it. It's not really like a dead mute. You just hit it, with a slight vibrato, and it'll bring it out and pick up the volume. You have a chord, and you put your palm right next to the bridge, and you hit it, and just forget about it. Then, you rely on the left hand—just a slight vibrato. Lots of times, it's so slight you don't even know there's a vibrato there, and the volume will come up.

I've never seen any other guitarist who could . . .

And now that I've figured out what it was, I'll never be able to do it again [*laughs*]. Most of the things I'm doing, I'm not even aware of what I'm playing. I know how to get the sounds, but I can't explain it to someone else. I've tried to teach other guys how to do it, but it wouldn't work for them like it did for me. It's the same with a lot of guys. If you asked Jimi Hendrix how he did all those things, I'll bet you a dollar to a nickel he couldn't have told you.

You also manipulate your tone control to produce a wah-wah effect. When did you figure that out?

When I was nine or ten and starting to play steel. I don't remember the name of the foot pedal steel players used back then, but you moved it up and down for volume, and side-to-side you had wah-wah. When I started to play a regular guitar, I did the same thing.

Have you ever used any mechanical devices like wah or fuzz?

Only before they came out. Like, to me, fuzz tone is only distortion, so I used to slice my speakers with razor blades, and soak them in water. I did that for a couple or three years. I was up in a session in New York one time, and I told a guy it was a shame they didn't have a device that would make distortion without doing that to your speakers. Then, about six years later, the fuzz tone came out. Mechanical devices can be a crutch, though. But some people, like Hendrix, Clapton, and Jeff Beck know how to use them effectively. I won't name any bad players.

What kind of amplifier do you use?

I was using a Fender Vibrolux with two ten-inch speakers. There was enough power there for me. If I had to play the Coliseum or something, I'd just mic it through another amp. I've tried most of the big ones, but they're not for me. They don't have the sound. They're good for feedback and so on, but I can't see much reason why you need all that power. Like I'll see some of these kids in a club that will seat maybe a hundred people, and they're up there with ten Marshalls—

wall-to-wall amplifiers—and the son-of-a-guns will be wide open. I can't see any reason for it.

Do you prefer any special brand of speakers or speaker set-up?

I know very little about electronics and different speakers. I just know when the sound is right. If I can get the right amplifier, I'm satisfied with the way the company makes the speakers. They know more about it than I do. But I do think some of the old instruments were better. I think they try to make them too perfect, and it ruins a lot of the good qualities—like the Magnetones. They've been changing them every year, but they've never equaled the old ones. And like Fender— you can't find much room to improve an old Fender Bassman. Even though they made a new one, I think the old ones are best. It's the same with guitars. The companies ought to wise up and reproduce the old ones. I remember when I used to go out and buy brand new Telecasters for $140. A white maple-neck Telecaster with case.

Roy, do you read music, or just pick tunes off the radio by ear?

Well, I don't read, and I don't listen to the radio. If I decide I want a new lick, I just lay in bed and think of it. Don't even need an instrument. Some of my best licks I can just think. Some of them aren't good, though, but when I try them out on the guitar, I know whether to keep them or not.

Why do you keep changing the structures of the songs you play over and over?

To keep it from getting monotonous. I may play them the same way, but I prefer to change them.

It was reported that you had your first solo album planned to come out in February 1971. What happened?

"DY-NO-MITE" DISCS!

Roy Buchanan, 1972

Second Album, 1974

A Street Called Straight, 1976

I canned it, because it was overdone. It had me sounding like too many other people—the Beatles, Cream, Hendrix—and I don't want to copy other cats. Everything I did on the first album was like show. I would go down to Nashville, and the tracks would already be made, and all I had to do was put the guitar part on. And they would sit there and say this is what we want you to put on it. Then, after I got through, I called the record company and told them I was dissatisfied. They asked if I thought I could do better, and I said, "Yes." So I made some dubs and sent them to them, and they said, "Okay, we'll do it your way." I want a little jazz, a little country, and a little blues.

Is there any particular musician you'd like to work with?

Yeah. Barney Kessel. He's great. I'd be ashamed to try to duplicate what he's doing in front of him, but I'd play my own thing. I've got some ideas of my own that would go along with his. I think jazz could be funkier, for one thing. It's possible to add jazz and rock together, in spite of what some people say. You just have to know how to do it.

Do you have any advice for young guitarists?

If I had it all to do over again, I'd probably learn to read music. And I'd spend more time practicing, and learning harmony and theory. The more you know about it, the better off you are. But also add your own things to it.

It has been said that if a man knows more about the theory of music, he would play different, with less feeling.

No, that's not true. The more knowledge you've got, the better you can do it. Sure, sometimes, you have to remember how you felt before, but it's a matter of using what you learn. If you can't do that, you might as well say you could play better 15 years ago than you can now. See what I mean? That's learning, too.

Eric Clapton. (COURTESY OF *GUITAR PLAYER* MAGAZINE)

BY FRED STUCKEY

JUNE 1970

Eric Clapton

SITTING IN BARE FEET ON THE EDGE OF A massive bed with a carved-wood headboard, Eric Clapton talked with *Guitar Player*. His soft-spoken manner made it difficult to hear his words clearly over the noise of conga drums and tourist chatter rising from Sausalito's main street. Eric's hotel room overlooked the park where so many of San Francisco's freaks and hip-types spend pleasant Marin County afternoons watching the tourists watch them.

With thin, sculptured fingers and fine, collar-length hair parted in the middle, Eric has the reserved bearing common to most Englishmen. He was born a quarter of a century ago to a working class family in a small town 30 miles south of London. Soon after his short-lived art school education, he was playing lead guitar for the Yardbirds. That was the beginning of a career that has netted Eric Clapton fame, fortune, and—strangely enough—humility. In the midst of the whirlwind madness of first-line appearances at San Francisco's Fillmore West and elsewhere, Eric has preserved a quiet dignity.

Eric left the Yardbirds to join John Mayall, England's foremost patron of American blues. He stayed with Mayall for two years. During that period, he mastered the blues idiom, and that training has been the cornerstone of the Clapton sound ever since. After the Mayall band, Eric got together with Jack Bruce and Ginger Baker. The result was the phenomenal Cream. Particularly for underground audiences, the Cream was a dynasty of sound. Through four unbelievable record albums and as many tours, no rock group had more charisma with audiences than the Cream. Cream followers were cultish in their enthusiasm. Eric's entrancingly sustained notes were an apex of rock-guitar solos.

Since the Cream, Eric formed and toured with Blind Faith, and has played guitar behind Delaney and Bonnie and the Beatles. He sings, plays guitar, and has written most of the tunes on a record album, *Eric Clapton Sings*, recorded in Los Angeles on the Atlantic label.

> **❝ I desperately try to think of something that will be effective, but I never sit down and work it out note for note. ❞**

When I saw you recently with Delaney and Bonnie, I noticed you weren't using the Les Paul you used with the Cream.

I still play a Les Paul. But with Delaney and Bonnie, I used an old Stratocaster I'd acquired. It's really, really good—a great sound. It's just right for the kind of bag I was playing with them.

Have you done anything to the Stratocaster—like modify the pickups, or have the frets shaved?

No. I just set the switch between the first and middle pickups. There is a little place where you can catch it so that you get a special sound somehow. I get much more rhythm and blues or rock kind of sound that way.

With the Cream you used big Marshall amps, right? Lately you've been using smaller Fender amps.

With Delaney and Bonnie, I used a Dual Showman—a big Fender amp. But I hardly ever jack it right up, you know. I'm not getting the sustain or holdover sound I used to get. It's still there a bit, but that's the Stratocaster.

When you played through those big Marshall amps with the Cream, would you turn them up to get that distorted, holdover sound?

Yeah. I'd turn the amp and the guitar up all the way. It seems I'm known as a guitar player for that sustain sound—you know, holding notes for a long time.

What kind of strings do you use on the Stratocaster?

Ernie Ball Super Slinky.

How about the strings you used on the Les Paul, on the live side of *Wheels of Fire*?

Fender Rock and Roll strings.

With the Cream, did you use more than one Marshall?

I had the option. I always had two Marshalls set up to play through. But, I think it was just so I could have one as a spare. I usually used only one 100-watt amp. I tried to use them in series several times—connected with a split lead—but it didn't work out too well. I would have one end of the cord going into the guitar and separating into the two amps. It was very hard to control and too loud, really.

What kind of wah-wah pedal do you use, like on the "White Room" track on *Wheels of Fire*?

Vox.

How do you typically set the volume and tone controls on your guitar and amp?

That depends on the guitar and amp. When I use the Stratocaster and Dual Showman, I have the pickup switch set between the first and middle pickups—which is a very bright sound, but not completely trebly. I take a little of the treble off, and I put on all of the bass and the middle. And I set the volume at about half.

Do you have a pick preference?

Yeah. Fender—the heavy ones. When I pick, I rest the butt or palm of my hand on the bridge of the guitar, and use it as a hinge or lever. When I stretch strings, I hook my thumb around the neck of the guitar. A lot of guitarists stretch strings with just their hand free. The only way I can do it is if I have my whole hand around the neck—actually gripping onto it with my thumb. That somehow gives me more of a rocking action with my hand and wrist.

Who were some of the blues people you listened to?

Oh, Robert Johnson for one. Of course, the way Robert Johnson played is very hard to accommodate into an electric-guitar style. The way Robert Johnson played was sort of a solo trip—it was an acoustic-guitar style. You can't really adapt it to the electric guitar very well without oversimplifying it. For guitar playing alone, there are a lot of people I like who didn't necessarily make it as solo blues artists. There was a guy called Tampa Red who was great, and there's Blind Willie Johnson who played slide guitar. He was fantastic—he played with a penknife. Most of them are dead and gone now.

Why did the Cream break up? It was the biggest group at the time. Who made that decision?

It was felt rather than decided. The tour before the last one was such a harrowing experience that we split from one another during it. We would hang out on our own with friends we had acquired in the cities we were in. We weren't living as a group at all. There was a lot of conflict.

How did the success of the Cream—all the hype and publicity—affect your attitude about things?

It made me very bitter indeed about being successful. When we first came here to play, that was when our egos really broke loose. Up until then, we were just an ordinary English, provincial group. We came to America, and the bubble burst. We thought we were God's gift. Then, we started to get put down by the press and so on, and I came down overnight. I think we all came down in the period of the tour preceding the farewell tour. It was just a question of working out the dates and getting back home so we could break it up.

Were you affected at all by playing as intensely and loudly with the Cream as you did?

I actually went deaf for a period of time. When we were playing at the Fillmore for a while, I was wearing specially designed ear plugs. I had to, because I couldn't hear anything anymore. I was playing full volume in a kind of weird, traumatic state—knowing that I had to play, and not really wanting to. I was deaf, and I couldn't hear anything. I was wearing these earplugs, and I couldn't hear through them. I was really brought down. I think one ear is stronger than the other. One ear is at least half deaf—I don't know which one. When I'm on stage, I have to stand a certain way to be able to hear everything. Otherwise, I can only hear half of what's going on.

How did the Delaney and Bonnie thing start?

It started on the Blind Faith tour. We had three or four days off at one time, and everybody from our group went home because they were homesick. I stayed, because I wanted to get into things here. I had no one else to hang out with, so I hung out with Delaney. He was very keen and everything. We started writing songs. And that was essentially more of a groove than it was to play with my own band. Blind Faith was going through all that hype stuff at the time. After the tour, I decided it would be nice to get together with them, and expose them a little more, and see if I could be of any help. Delaney gave me a lot of confidence to be able to sing.

After the Cream, you got together with Ginger Baker and Steve Winwood in Blind Faith. What did you think of the Blind Faith experience?

It wasn't quite what Steve and I had hoped it would be. We started out with very big ideas about it, and gradually it started to lose the original kind of concept of what we were going to do. Finally, we were just living up to our commitments—just doing the tour and playing the album. It didn't come off as well as we had intended. Our names got in the way—you know, all that supergroup hype. The best stuff we did was when we were just jamming at Steve's place, or at my house. We have tapes of that, which are just hours of instrumental, fun-type jazz things. That's what Blind Faith was all about, but it was never exposed to the public. When we came to do the tour, we were so nervous about playing in front of that many people—with all that hype going down—that we just tried to be as professional as possible. We played the album, and tried to do an act. We didn't make it on that level.

Do you plan your leads, or, for that matter, do you plan them now?

No. The only planning I do is about a minute before I play. I desperately try to think of something that will be effective, but I never sit down and work it out note for note.

You usually don't build your solos around a theme riff.

I might, say, if the song is a very popular one. Like when I played "Sunshine of Your Love" with the Cream, I'd play something like what I

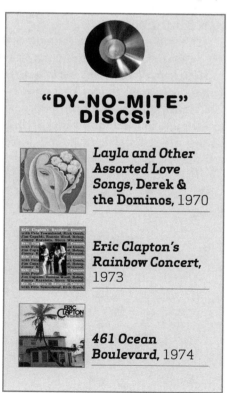

"DY-NO-MITE" DISCS!

Layla and Other Assorted Love Songs, Derek & the Dominos, 1970

Eric Clapton's Rainbow Concert, 1973

461 Ocean Boulevard, 1974

laid down on the record. I'd hint at it, but not necessarily repeat it.

Have you heard other guitarists around playing what are obviously your runs?

I do sometimes think that, but it's probably just conceit on my part. There's no reason why I should think that—seeing as how I copied most of my runs from B. B. or Albert King or Freddie King. There's no reason why they should listen to me, when they can listen to the masters—you know, the source.

By the way, was that you playing the lead guitar part on "While My Guitar Gently Weeps" on the Beatles album? There were some rumors that you took George Harrison's place on that track.

That was me. George and I were doing something the day he was to record that track. He had to go down to the studio that day, and cut the track with the rest of the group. They were all waiting for him, and he wanted me to play the guitar on the cut because he thought he couldn't do it the way he wanted to hear it. I didn't agree with him. I thought he should have played guitar on it, but it was great for me to do it. We agreed that I wouldn't get paid for it, or have my name mentioned.

Did you use your Les Paul on that track?

Yeah, the Les Paul through a Marshall amp.

You know, it surprises me in a way that you've kept your head together after having played for so long with so many heavy, heavy bands.

Well, I've lost a lot of it. I've lost a lot of the peace of mind I used to have. It can be acquired again, but it takes a concentrated effort at being still and staying at home. I'm not too keen on too much more touring. I'd like to take a holiday.

Roots-music disciple Ry
Cooder. (COURTESY OF
GUITAR PLAYER MAGAZINE)

BY MICHAEL PIERCE

Ry Cooder

INSTRUMENTS: BOTTLENECK GUITAR, MANDOLIN, banjo.

Credits: Rolling Stones, Taj Mahal, Captain Beefheart, Paul Revere and the Raiders, Harpers Bizarre, Everly Brothers.

Born: Los Angeles, 1947.

Dug: Woody Guthrie, Burl Ives, Josh White.

Career: Played Los Angeles clubs with Jackie DeShannon, introduced to bottleneck by John Fahey, became expert in bottleneck history, then joined Taj's first band, and later Beefheart and others.

Solo recording: *Ry Cooder*, released October 1970.

Who were some of the people you first listened to when you started playing?

The first slide guitarist I heard—and the most impressive—was Robert Johnson. At that time, I was playing Merle Travis stuff, and somebody told me to listen to Johnson's music because it was great and different. I actually heard Blind Willie Johnson first, but I didn't have any idea what he was doing. The fact he was playing with a slide didn't even occur to me. So they started reissuing all these records by people like Charlie Patton, Blind Willie, and Robert Johnson, and I began concentrating on them. Soon, I stopped fingerpicking, and I started playing slide.

Guitar PLAYER

Annual Artist Issue
Jerry Reed Carlos
Montoya John Lee
Hooker Ry Cooder
Jerry Hahn Buddy
Merrill Pentangle
Hoyt Axton Dave
Van Ronk & '71 Poll

It has been said that you studied slide with John Fahey.

I didn't actually take lessons. I knew him, and he'd sit around and play what he was learning. He'd put together this whole thing on how it's done—not so much the idea of the notes, but the entire movement of the thing. The guy is encyclopedic with stuff about the blues. When I watched him play, I saw that this was a guy who knew how to move his hands. He was getting the feeling when most people were frantically playing 30,000 notes. I saw him play bottleneck twice, so I figured out the visual thing, put that together with what I was hearing on the records, and began to make a sound.

Do you consider yourself basically a blues, folk or country player?

I don't even like to be thought of as a country player. I studied it, but not to play it. I just like the music, the feeling, and the harmonies. I never learned to flatpick country guitar, and Travis picking was a dead-end street. Once you learn it, it's like pre-programmed stuff. My feelings are really in blues and old jazz.

You spent a lot of time in studios over the years. How do you approach that whole scene?

You have to approach that thing as a group effort. In other words, I'm not in any way visionary. Whatever I play in the studio, I don't really know what it sounds like, so I'm inclined to say that it sounds bad. I can't tell what I'm doing. If somebody said something was good, and I trusted that person, after a lot of dickering around, I would probably say, "Okay." So for one thing, you need help to really assess what you're doing. I don't think you can do it all by yourself. I sure can't. And the more expert advice you get, the luckier you are.

Given the fact that most recording studios are sterile, how do you loosen up?

You just play your way through it. A lot of people get bogged down with that. But, actually, it's not a bad place to be, because you've got a lot of possibilities. You can do damn near anything you want to in a studio, and that's nice. It's encouraging. If you have a good engineer, you have a lot of help from that standpoint. There are a lot of things that can be done, and you can really stretch out—*if* you can do it psychologically, which I can have a pretty tough time doing. I don't mind the sterility of it so much. Studios are pretty much clean, so they're not distracting in any way. They feel like a place to work—no nonsense. I like that. There's a lot of pressure there, and that's good, too, because working under pressure gets results.

Could you rap a little bit about the instruments you have?

For acoustic guitars, I'll always use a Martin. Right now, I have a real turnip. It's the new D-45, and it's not very good. It has green wood, and it weighs a ton. It has a nice mellow sound if you're playing very quietly. It's a good recording guitar, but a bad picking guitar, because you can't hear it when you play.

I'd like to have a great guitar—like a really old Martin—but I don't collect instruments, because I don't know that much about them. I don't work on them myself like a lot of people do, so maybe that's the problem. If I could work on them myself, I could adjust them and make them just so. I could take it to a guy, but I don't trust any of them in Los Angeles, because what do they know about what I want?

The Stratocaster I have is practically brand new. It's about five years old, and it's completely unmodified. I just have the action raised up and leveled out, and I tried to have as much of the curve taken out of the bridge so the slide would work on it. I have real heavy, Fender flatwound medium-gauge strings on it. They're just the big jazz strings. The Fender is my favorite instrument for electrics, because it has got the punch. I've also got a Gibson ES-335. It has got a funny thing. Something is wrong with the wiring on the pickups, but it has a great sound because of that. And the trouble with those guitars is that the bass strings just do not fret true, and I don't know what to do about it. But I like it. I like the neck.

> **I think that bottleneck is unique in that it has the same quality as the human voice.**

What do you use for a slide?

A vinegar bottle. It's just because it's straight. Most bottles today have a curve, and they're useless. I don't like the sound that metal slides get. They get harsh. I like the glass, because it feels a little softer, a little lighter. Maybe it's just that the metal is so slick. It lacks texture, I think. The glass is a rough finish—even though it's smooth—and it does have a feel if you play slow. With the metal, you can't control the texture of a note. You have just one quality all the time. If you slide up slowly, you just get a steady, almost electronic sound. I think maybe it's also psychological. It's probably because I associate glass with all the old guys.

What tunings do you use?

I use *G*, open *G*, and one that I don't know whether you call it *E* or *D* tuning. I use it to play in *D* or *E*, depending where my capo is. I like the *E* tuning best, because it's rich. I like *G*, because it seems that a lot of things fall right into place. You can do Robert Johnson–type stuff. "Honky Tonk Women" is in *G* tuning, and I like to play that once in a while.

What do you feel are the unique characteristics of the bottleneck guitar?

I think that bottleneck is unique in that it has the same quality as the human voice. What Blind Willie Johnson did that was real striking, was to play melodies with the bottleneck just as he would sing them. And that's another thing that people have done—they play and sing, and then instead of finishing the verse, they play the last line with the bottleneck. So it does have the quality of the voice. It sustains, and because you're not fretting notes, you can play any melody you want if you know your tuning well enough. It all depends on your technique. If you are messing around a fret, you're not going to get a good note. But if you practice long enough, you're going to get accuracy, and that's the first thing.

When you say accuracy, you mean playing right on the fret like a steel player?

Right on the fret. It's the same principle as steel, so you need the accuracy. And once you can do that, you can express the note by either vibrato, or by sliding into the note. It's all up to you after that—how you want to express the notes. Bottleneck can be very expressive, which is what I like most about it.

Getting more into the record-company ideology, is there as much hype with the major labels as is popularly believed?

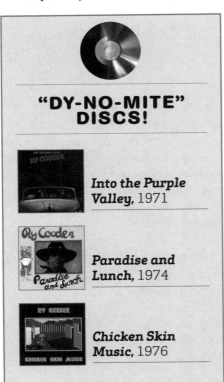

"DY-NO-MITE" DISCS!

Into the Purple Valley, 1971

Paradise and Lunch, 1974

Chicken Skin Music, 1976

Right. They need the sales: "Beautiful trip, man, but we need the sales. Are we going to merchandise the situation, or aren't we going to merchandise the situation?" I hear that all the time. Fortunately, I have been able to get acquainted with the people in distribution at Warner Brothers/Reprise—you know, the promotion guys, the special project guys, the radio guys—and they like me well enough. I'm really just trying to make a living. If it's units to them, it's a job to me.

Larry Coryell puts some glam style into his jazz. (© MICHAEL PUTLAND/ RETNA LTD.)

BY MICHAEL BROOKS

DECEMBER 1974

Larry Coryell

FEW GUITARISTS HAVE THE ABILITY TO SPEAK as palpably through the instrument as Larry Coryell—though that was never enough to blast him to the top of some commercial chart. Playing a '60s rock-and-blues style that evolved into a jazz-flavored blend with such notables as Chico Hamilton, Gary Burton, and his own groups, Coryell has never had a hit. But what he does have is respect from his peers, and—at his level of musicianship—that in itself is an accomplishment.

Fronting his own band, the Eleventh House, which features Alphonse Mouzon on drums, Danny Trifan on bass, Mike Mandel on keyboards, and Mike Lawrence on trumpet, Larry continues to mesh the energy of rock with the intricacies of jazz.

At the present time, he is using a Hagstrom Swede electric (strung with Dan Armstrong strings) through a Sound City SMF Tour Series amp and a Mu-Tron III. For acoustic work, Coryell has chosen a LoPrinzi LR-l 5 dreadnaught.

How is your music in live sets as far as improvisation versus set patterns?

We're a lot looser live than the rather restricted format we put down for *Introducing the Eleventh House*. I'm not criticizing the format that limited the solos and kept them short,

because that's probably the reason for the album's success. The album really gave a lot of my old fans and many newcomers a clear and concise sampler of what was there. Everybody got a chance to stretch out on the record, and yet there were no egotistical masturbations—with the exception of myself. I had to give myself a long solo to establish the fact that I'm a little out front.

When we first got this thing together, Mose [Mouzon] and I had a long talk over the phone, and we both agreed that the old way of total freedom both inside and outside the structure was no good anymore. We felt that we had to build the structure, and then do the freedom within the structure. If the structure was strong enough, the freedom *within* the structure would give us enough freedom to do what we wanted.

Where did you get the idea for this structured freedom approach?

One man—whose name is Anthony Armando "Chick" Corea. About a year ago, our old band played opposite him, and he blew us off the stage. I felt it was because Chick had that tight ensemble thing to contrast with the freedom of the jazz. And I said, "Okay, he's winning and I'm losing, and I can see why." I didn't walk up to him and say "thanks," but in my mind I did. He made me realize that freedom is only reached through the structure.

In your August 1970 interview with *GP*, you said you liked to play flashy, and then you were hipped by Gábor Szabó that music is first, and the instrument is second.

I remember that. Up to the time I had met Gábor, I was just out to impress people with my guitar playing. He made me realize that I just wanted to impress people with the music that was in me, and it just wasn't coming out because I was trying to impress people. But Gábor wasn't the only guy who had made that statement. A long time ago, Barney Kessel mentioned that his instrument was only an instrument—merely the means to an end. At that time, I was in my teens, and I really didn't understand it. Then, when I was playing with Gábor up in Seattle around 1965, he like really hit me with that, and it made a very strong impact. From then on, I tried to change my philosophy to make music first. But I also know that very often I will fall back into "guitaristics," and I accept it.

It seems to me that in order to be a good musician, you have got to have a fairly high ego?

No way. Django Reinhardt was the most humble cat, and Jim Hall is extremely modest.

But each projects his ego differently.

Well, I think what they are projecting is the music that comes out of the cosmos and out of the earth, and they just allow themselves to be an antenna. All this music is in the earth, in the sky, and it comes through some people—their bodies, their hands, and their instruments. Needless to say, you've got to have some ego just to check into a motel, but ego is a double-edged sword. You can either fill a house with it, or cut yourself. And I think if you use ego properly, that's good. The ego is what you think about yourself, and because what you think about yourself can be so inconsistent with what other people think about you, to rely on your own egocentricity is very dangerous. I found myself patting myself on the back after playing some of the things I did, and I said, "Wait a minute—what am I bragging about?" I think it's better to consider yourself just an instrument, and if there's any credit due, it's not due to you or your ego, it's just due to the circumstances you're in. You know, there are a lot of weird guitar players—jazz guitarists in their 30s, 40s, and 50s—who owe everything they play to Charlie Christian and Django Reinhardt. Even though these guys went much further financially, they really copped it from Charlie and Django. Music is everybody's property, though.

Did you get into jazz because of its difficulty?

It's really hard to do an imitation of a Charlie Parker solo, but, by the same token, it's not that easy to do an imitation of Eric Clapton when he was on the *Bluesbreakers* trip. You can get the solo, but to get that vibrato is something else.

What I'm really asking is, did you come on to jazz because it was more of a challenge than a musical pursuit?

I don't know what the difference is. I just did it. As a teenager, I would listen to Wes Montgomery, and just not have any idea how he did it. Not the technique—but his mind. His really great solos like "West Coast Blues" just blew me out, so I learned that very solo myself. Not because I wanted to play like Wes—because that would be like asking a Ford to be like a Rolls Royce—but just to understand how his mind worked to get those ideas. After studying all those Wes Montgomery solos, I started to get one or two ideas about how to think. For example, if he was playing a blues in *C*, instead of thinking *C* as he was starting to do his chorus, he would think *Bb minor 7*, and that's how he would get his modernness. And that would lead into suspensions of *Bb* triads over *C*.

What was really incredible was in "West Coast Blues" where he would play a straight blues over the head, and then for a change after he got to the four chord, he would go to the four-minor, to the sharp sixth, seventh, and then the third-minor, to the straight six, seven, and then chromatically down to the two-minor chord, into the five. Then, instead of going straight to the one, Wes played that beautiful thing that went to the $B\flat$ to $D\flat$ to $G\flat$ to B. It's just a progression like you find on early be-bop things, and it's also a variation of the I-II-VI-V progressions you find in rock music.

How did you take to the odd meters of jazz?

If you want to talk about odd meters, man, Mahavishnu's John McLaughlin was a great breakthrough. He really put everything in odd meters, played rock within that structure, and woke up the entire non-jazz public.

Do you feel jazz will one day be popular, mass-media entertainment?

Not general-public entertainment. But I do think that rock, with its one-chord, two-chord songs is boring people to tears. Jazz, though, goes beyond music—it's enlightenment. The real point of jazz goes beyond entertainment. There's a big difference between performing and creating, and I feel the really great jazz performers—even though as a sidelight they may be entertaining—feel it is their duty to create.

Some people think the idea in jazz is to cook more than create.

Cooking is a creative thing. You can get down there and play four-four, but if you're not cooking, you're not creating. The Beatles would go

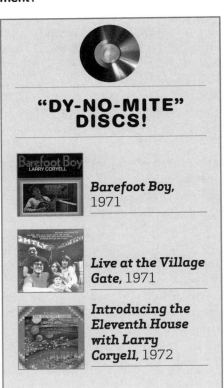

"DY-NO-MITE" DISCS!

Barefoot Boy, 1971

Live at the Village Gate, 1971

Introducing the Eleventh House with Larry Coryell, 1972

"twing, twing, twang" and everybody would scream, and it was great. But now, especially when young people are a whole lot more sophisticated, I think people are looking for enlightenment—not escape. I loved to escape with Donovan and all those people, but I think the times have changed now, and I think that enlightenment is just one degree beyond that musical escape that gripped our musical fabric.

When you practice guitar, do you play a lot of scales?

Hell, yes—it's the basis of all music. Whenever I practice, I start out with simple scales, and then I move on to the more complicated ones.

Did you develop your speed through exercises, or by just playing the music?

Through exercises, for sure. I can't think of anything other than just doing it over and over. The real thing about speed, though, is when you can create at that high level. Tal Farlow does that real well.

How do you relate most of your exercises to your lead playing?

When I'm improvising, I'm not conscious of anything I do. I'm all heart, and I try to turn the mind off. But when I'm practicing, it's all mind.

Can you do that all the time?

You have to, or else you'll never improvise a note. You have to practice to use your mind in the woodshed in order to free your mind when you're up there on stage.

What is your future as a guitarist?

My future is just to be the eternal student—to continue developing my flow of ideas with my ability to flow with them. My calling on this planet is to be a searcher—in search of something new. But I won't be disappointed if on the day I die I don't find it. At least, I'll be searching.

No, it's not Leather Tuscadero—it's Rick Derringer. (COURTESY OF *GUITAR PLAYER* MAGAZINE)

BY DON MENN

AUGUST 1975

Rick Derringer

LITTLE NINE-YEAR-OLD RICK ZEHRINGER, WITH wide lapels, slicked-back hair, and a bow tie, staring out of some mirror of the past facing his own future, would have been hard put to recognize the form he has taken today as Rick Derringer—rock guitarist, song-writer, and producer for himself, as well as for such luminaries as Johnny and Edgar Winter, the Osmond Brothers, Richie Havens, Steely Dan, Todd Rundgren, and Alice Cooper. Squinting wouldn't help young Zehringer recognize his new form. Little in his life is the same.

His audiences, for example. Rick, at nine, was strumming country-western ditties for the dozing town fathers of Fort Recovery, Ohio, at their Kiwanis and Rotary Club luncheons. Today, nearly two decades later, Derringer is electrifying the whole world's sons and daughters that storm the stages of rock and roll halls everywhere he goes.

Instruments, too, have come and gone. He has owned everything from a white, three-pickup Supro ("Now that was a hot-looking guitar!") to a rare Explorer, which is the visual counterpart of the custom instrument he now uses on stage.

Today, Derringer can hardly recall

the titles from his parents' large record collection, which he describes as "a lot of country-western records, a lot of '50s music, and not too much rock."

His influences have changed, as well. His first was an uncle in Michigan who played in bars. Rick's musical drive was encouraged by his parents, who were willing to take him into bars to listen to the local guitarists. Today, though his primary interest is rock and roll, he tries to catch as many different kinds of acts as possible, including jazz.

Perhaps this avidness is Rick's most noticeably consistent quality. He has always learned from everyone he could.

"Every time I'd meet a guitar player," he recalls, "I'd get him to show me something."

When he was 15, he moved to Union City, Indiana, and expanded his musical skills by learning snare drum, tympani, and bass while he was playing rhythm guitar in the high school swing band. During this time, the McCoys was formed—a trio that went through numerous changes of its own, alternately known as the McCoys, the Rick Z. Combo, Rick and the Raiders, and back again to the McCoys. One song, "Hang On Sloopy," catapulted the group to fame. Within a month after its release, it was number one in almost every country in the world.

An up-and-down career kept the McCoys visible, but a bit seasick, until Steve Paul made them house band for his club, the Scene, and the backup band for Johnny Winter. To avoid further mispronunciation, misspelling, and misplacement, Zehringer changed his professional name to "Derringer" on the *Johnny Winter And* album. It has stuck throughout his subsequent work with Edgar Winter, and is the name that appears on his own solo albums, the latest of which is *Spring Fever*.

What were your first guitars?

When I was about five years old, I got a Stella acoustic guitar as a kind of a toy. I didn't know that you could make music with it, because I wasn't really interested in it too much. My brother and I used to play with it a lot, and paint our names on it, like country-western guys did. I must have been about eight when we finally culminated our whole experience with it by stomping on it, and breaking it into shreds [*laughs*]. Right after that, I realized that my uncle was a guitarist, and I got interested in playing the guitar myself. Then, for my ninth birthday, I got what I really consider my first guitar. It didn't really have a brand name on it, but it was an electric, one pickup, gold-painted guitar. And at the same time, I got a sleazy Gibson amp—I think it had one 12" speaker in it—but it was great, because most parents, especially at that time before guitars were fads, for sure wouldn't go out and get a brand new electric guitar and an electric amp. After I got that guitar, I learned everything I could about it. From then on, I was always trying to get a better guitar. I've always been a collector—zillions of guitars.

Did you get your first licks off of records?

Not at all. When I first started, I didn't know you were supposed to learn specific licks. I didn't know anything about that kind of stuff. I was just into learning how to play the guitar. Electric guitars were just starting to become more of an "in" thing in rock and roll when I was nine, and, in fact, the guitar was very seldom heard as a solo instrument. On the same day I got the guitar, my dad found out that a mechanic named Gene Feilly at Ford Garage in Fort Recovery, Ohio—where I lived at that time—played guitar. Gene was just exactly the way you'd picture a mechanic to be—a great big guy with pockmarks all over his face, and dirt all over his work clothes. But

> 66 I just try to use everything I've heard in order to come up with music that fits whatever I'm playing. 99

he was the kindest, most gentle, jolly kind of mechanic all the time. I went down to his house and said, "I just got this guitar, and I know you don't know me, but could you show me something on it?" So he showed me an open-G chord, and a D chord, and showed me some ways to use them. I went home and played those chords probably a thousand times that night, and went right back the next day to try to learn more. That's basically how I got started—just learning chords. You see, soloing was not why I got involved with playing—it was to be a part of music. And that meant playing rhythm and chords.

What's your studio and stage setup?

On stage, I use an Ampeg SVT amp and two 4x12 cabinets loaded with Altec speakers.

Where do you set the tone and volume on the amp?

The volume is at about two o'clock. For tone, the high switch is on, and the treble is set to three o'clock, midrange to twelve o'clock, and the bass at three o'clock. That won't work for all guitars, because my guitar is a little brighter and a little louder than most.

What guitars are you using?

The ones I'm using onstage are made by Charlie LoBue at Guitar Lab in New York City. I didn't want to take the chance of getting my real Gibson Explorer stolen, so I asked Charlie to make one that was similar—maybe even a little better. So an Explorer copy it's not—it's an Explorer body style. The humbucking pickups are rewound with a little better gauge copper wire, and, supposedly, a little better magnet. All 12 poles are bored out, and screws are inserted so that they can be raised as high to the strings as possible. That creates a real loud, good-sounding guitar. It also has some binding where Explorers didn't, and the body is made from birch. That's a real hard, heavy wood, so it had to be a little smaller than the Explorer in thickness, but it produces a little more treble. This guitar is also different because it has a Schaller bridge, which offers more travel for adjusting the intonation. I adjust the intonation every time I change the strings, or at least I check it.

What sort of strings are you using?

Ernie Ball Super Slinky with an unwound third. I change strings about every three shows. In the studio, a string will last longer.

Do you practice systematically?

Yeah. I do all kinds of stuff—chromatic scales, major scales, whole-tone fifth scales, and whatever keeps my fingers moving and loose, so they don't freeze up on me. Of course, I also learn solos note for note from records, and because of that, I learn plenty of licks. I just try to use everything I've heard in order to come up with music that fits whatever I'm playing.

Do you ever work for an improvisational feel during performance?

A lot. But I feel people would like to hear some solos like they hear them on the radio, so I just play the solos from hits exactly as they were on the original versions. On other songs, I approach the solos as improvisational sections.

Where do you get your licks?

It probably started out from knowing a combination of chord structures, patterns, and scales. I try all the time to become totally fluent on the instrument. In other words, some people can create exactly what comes into their minds instantaneously with their voice. In my mind, the ideal point to get to on the guitar is where you don't have to think about scales, keys, notes, harmonic structures—none of that stuff. You can just play music fluently.

What about your pick?

Right now, I'm using these heavy, triangular-shaped ones made by Pastore.

Do you play slide?

Yeah. I play in a standard open-*E* tuning. I use a metal bar on my little finger so I can play with my other fingers. I used to get them made at a plumbing shop, because that was a heavier bar, and I could get exactly the size I wanted for my finger, and have it polished down real nice. But those always get lost or stolen, so now I'm just using a bar like you get in a music store. They're a little big for my finger, so I put masking tape inside until it's actually kind of form fitted to my finger.

Johnny [Winter] showed me a lot, and I played slide a lot in the McCoys, as well. One time, in fact, Johnny and I were with Duane Allman, and I thought, "Here I am, a young kid playing with these guys who have been into country blues all their lives." At one point, Duane said, "By the way, I've been meaning to tell you that I came down when you were at the Image in Miami. You were playing slide guitar on some song, and I just wanted to tell you that you were the person who made me think, 'Wow, that slide can make some real good rockin' music.'" I had thought Duane was interested in slide all his life, but here he is, telling me that I was one of the people who made him become more involved with slide guitar. I only used it on one lousy song, and here Duane is telling me all this, and he becomes real famous for slide guitar. I loved it.

How do you get your vibrato?

I hadn't heard anything about Django Reinhardt records where he was bending strings, so I just didn't know anything about it. But, eventually, I learned, and it was

"DY-NO-MITE" DISCS!

Roadwork, Edgar Winter's White Trash, 1972

All American Boy, 1974

Live, 1974

really hard for me to develop vibrato, because I'd never done it. For a while, my vibrato was too fast. It's hard to slow it down. I do it all different, but never with the little finger. I always use one of the first three fingers. I bend down only if I'm playing one of the low strings, and would run out of neck if I bent up.

What sort of pedals and devices do you use?

On stage, I use a Vox wah-wah and an MXR phaser. That's it. In the studio, it's anything I can find, and everything that I like. I go up to Manny's Music in New York City, and try to discover new gadgets and gimmicks that sound cool, but that people haven't heard too much.

Was there an abrupt change in your musical growth after "Hang On Sloopy" started you touring?

Touring is one of the ways you actually get better at playing the guitar—at least for me. Before "Hang On Sloopy," there was always the temptation to play music that didn't really develop my dexterity as a musician. At home, I have a tendency to play real simple music, or music I like that I may have played many times before. On the road, it's a different kind of thing, because you're on stage trying to impress people, as well as play good music. I look at playing on the road as real good practice. If you've done a song enough times, you don't have to worry about remembering it—a framework is established. Now, you can use that song as a vehicle to create, because you're playing something you know so well that you can consider new things to do with it.

Al Di Meola unleashes one of his melodically complex and frighteningly fast guitar solos. (COURTESY OF *GUITAR PLAYER* MAGAZINE)

BY JIM CROCKETT

OCTOBER 1975

Al Di Meola

THE NAMES OF CHICK COREA AND STANLEY Clarke are well known to all followers of contemporary rock and jazz as the creators of Chick's popular band, Return to Forever. But increasingly, since the departure of lead guitarist Bill Connors late last year, the name Al Di Meola is becoming a watchword among young guitar players. After all, to have joined Return to Forever at 19, you've got to have chops.

Di Meola was born in Jersey City, New Jersey, but raised close by in Bergenfield. While his parents weren't musical, they did encourage their son in the field, even buying him a set of drums when Al was only five. Three years later, the youngster got his first guitar ("I had just heard my initial taste of the Beatles and Elvis"), and by then he was playing electric.

In the fifth grade, Al fronted his first band, organizing another one later in high school. While he liked listening to rock and roll, it wasn't a style he enjoyed playing. He recalls that at 14, "I went to Greenwich Village, Fillmore East, places like that. I bought all the records I could get—all the Frisco bands like Santana, I got the Who, and just about everybody. I'd sit in my room hour after hour getting the tunes down. I really liked the rhythm more than the lead."

Two years later, Di Meola was into country music, sporting cowboy clothes and playing bluegrass. He even bought a pedal steel, almost giving up standard guitar altogether. Al says, "I had to decide to try and master one, since I knew I couldn't devote myself totally to both instruments. I loved jazz, but was completely wiped out by Buddy Emmons, Rusty Young, and Al Perkins, and realized that I could never play steel that well."

Di Meola loved the way the late Clarence White played with the Byrds, and admits that he and Jerry Garcia were among his biggest influences at the time. But at 16, the young guitarist heard his first Larry Coryell album, *Fairyland*.

"Man, it really knocked me out," he says. "It was what I always wanted to do."

Between his six years of country guitar, rock guitar, and some jazz, Di Meola's technique was well enough together so that the idea of one day playing with a band like Larry's wasn't too far from possibility.

Al was still fronting a country band, but twice a week would rush to New York clubs like Village Gate and Slugs to catch Coryell. "I even went to Larry's Pennsylvania farm a few times," Al remembers. "We'd jam together, and he gave me all kinds of tips. He really inspired me, and he'd give me lots of encouragement—like telling me I was fantastic. He introduced me around to other people in the field, too. I'd go home feeling great—ready to learn as much as I could."

Al was now buying all the jazz albums he could afford—especially John McLaughlin, trumpeter Miles Davis, and tenor saxman John Coltrane.

"I didn't dig Chick all that much then, though," Di Meola insists. "He was into a free thing, and I hated it. But because I knew he had played with Miles, I went to the Village Vanguard to hear him. Man, I came away tingling."

This was Corea's first Return to Forever with Clarke on bass, singer Flora Purim, and Airto on percussion. A year later, Chick would re-form the band without a singer, but with Bill Connors playing guitar.

After high school, Di Meola went to Berklee College of Music in Boston to major in Instrumental Performance (he admits, though, that he has since forgotten most of the technical knowledge he gained there).

"The schooling was very inspirational, but I haven't worried about remembering it all. All I play now I really got on my own. But inspiration is the key to learning, so in that way the semester and a half I spent at Berklee was a good investment."

In college, while Forever was Al's favorite group, he listened mostly to the Barry Miles Quintet with another young guitar player, John Abercrombie. After a chance visit to Lakewood, New Jersey, where Barry's band was playing, Al's friend, Mike Buykukas, arranged for an audition at New York's Bitter End. So at 18, Di Meola left school to join Barry Miles. The tenure lasted six months, and included working with Eric Kloss and the Neophonic Orchestra performing a Kloss suite on television. There really wasn't enough work, though, so it was back to Berklee to study arranging.

Re-enter Mike Buykukas. Al explains: "Mike had some tapes of me when I was with the Barry Miles band, and he kept taking them to Chick's apartment, trying to get Chick to listen to them. Mike must have spent a hundred dollars on calls to Chick, urging him to listen to the tapes. Finally, he just went to the apartment and almost refused to leave until the tapes were checked out."

Chick auditioned the tapes, and flipped. He called Di Meola in Boston in July 1974, to join Return to Forever, and Al couldn't believe it.

"It was my favorite group, and here I was joining it without even a tryout," Al says. "To me, there was nothing else. In 15 minutes I was packed. I got a ride with a friend, and I haven't seen that apartment since."

But the pressure was now on. There were just two days until the band's sold-out Carnegie Hall concert. For ten hours a day, the group rehearsed Chick's intricate tunes. Di Meola made it (reading the high-energy charts on stage), and the band got unanimous rave reviews. The next night, they were in Atlanta before 40,000 people (prior to joining Forever, Al's largest audience was 600). From then on, it has been one success after another, one hit album after another, and today Di Meola's name is as well known to *GP*'s readers as Chick's is to those of *Contemporary Keyboard*.

Al's first guitar was an acoustic Tempo, the second a Japanese electric.

"The first real good guitar I had," he feels, "was a Guild Starfire in the seventh grade. With the import, I used a Danelectro amp, but with the Guild, I went to a Bandmaster."

After four years with the Starfire, Di Meola switched to a Les Paul Custom, made for him at the factory (stereo with Varitone). In the meantime, Al went to the Alembic company to re-wire it, add some shielding, and remove the Bigsby tailpiece.

His amp today is a 1958 Fender Twin Reverb with two Gilsonite (of Englewood, New Jersey) bottoms. Each cabinet contains four 12" EBM speakers made by Electro-Voice.

Consistent with the Corea utilization of electronic sounds, Di Meola has added an Edwards volume pedal and a Colorsound wah-wah. But that's not all. There is also a Maestro four-range booster with added fuzz, plus a foot-operated Taurus synthesizer made by Moog ("It utilizes a sub-harmonic switch that I use to get sounds an octave lower").

On the Les Paul, Al uses Dan Armstrong Ultra Light strings with a .008 for the first, and an unwound third. Di Meola also plays an Ovation Balladeer acoustic/electric ("I don't like the electric sound, though, so I just play it as an acoustic"), using it for the band's occasional all-acoustic numbers. He strings the Ovation with Guild Spanish Lights. On the Balladeer, Di Meola uses a Gilsonite heavy pick, but switches to their medium gauge for the electric.

The Al Di Meola technique is a mixture of various habits he has picked up over the years. He does his rhythmic strumming from the wrist for greater flexibility, but anchors his palm on the guitar bridge for the stability he needs during the lightning solos for which he is so well known. And when he needs a more mellow coloration, he picks closer to the bass pick-up, and slides his pick toward the bridge when he wants a treble sound.

When he adds fingerpicking to his solos it's with the first two fingers. For fretting, Al utilizes all his fingers, but not the thumb ("It's really frustrating to see so many rockers using only their first and third fingers to fret with—it's so limiting to eliminate half of your hand").

When the band performs such favorites as "Vulcan

"DY-NO-MITE" DISCS!

Where Have I Known You Before, Return to Forever, 1974

Land of the Midnight Sun, 1976

Elegant Gypsy, 1977

Worlds" and "Where Have I Known You Before" in concert, guitarists in the audience are always astounded by Al's effective percussive, staccato sound during parts of the tunes. This he achieves by muting the strings with his right-hand palm while he solos, a technique he developed years ago in an effort to soften the sound of his amp.

Di Meola's influences have been as varied as they are talented—from composers such as Stravinsky, to non-guitarists like pianist Herbie Hancock, Miles, and Coltrane, and from such jazz guitar players as Ralph Towner, Larry Coryell, and John McLaughlin to the classical guitarist Julian Bream and the flamenco master Serranito.

"The best tip I could give," Di Meola advises, "is to find an influence or two—some players you really favor—and listen to them the majority of the time. Try to pick up on what they're doing. Get every album they're on, and see them play whenever you can. Then, apply what they're doing to what you want to play. Soon enough, you'll discard most of the other people's licks and techniques in favor of your own; and that, after all, is the goal."

José Feliciano owned *Guitar Player*'s "Best Pop Guitarist" award in the '70s. (COURTESY OF *GUITAR PLAYER* MAGAZINE)

José Feliciano

*T*HESE QUESTIONS WERE SUBMITTED BY *Roger Edens of Columbus, Ohio.*

What type of classical guitar do you use? What type would you recommend for students?

Right now, I am using two brands. I'm using a Candelas, made in Los Angeles, California. The guitar maker's name is Candelario Delgado. The other is made in Brazil—it's a Giannini. I highly recommend this guitar for students. It is an excellent guitar. In fact, it is a student model. For me to recommend a product, I must really be interested in it. I cannot be pressured into saying something I do not believe.

I noticed on your last album that you play electric guitar. What type of electric guitar do you use?

Well, I have played all kinds. I was looking for a Les Paul, but they ran out. However, I found an electric guitar which I think beats them all. It's a Vox, and it has all sorts of effects built into it—like fuzz and wah-wah.

Do you cut your fingernails on your right hand?

No. I just file them, and get them straightened out.

Your style seems to be a curious blend of Latin and flamenco techniques. Which is the more influential?

I don't feel any flamenco tech-

nique in my playing. The thing is that I use the same finger strokes that flamenco players use. This I sort of learned on my own, and I also learned from a guitar teacher at the age of 17. They had what they called classical training, but I had learned everything on my own—including my technique. I was doing other things, and my hands were kind of backwards in the things I was playing. So I had to get a teacher to straighten out my technique. I had a very fine guitar teacher, Harold Morris, in New York City. I learned classical pieces from him, and he also taught me jazz.

> ❝ They had what they called classical training, but I had learned everything on my own—including my technique. ❞

"DY-NO-MITE" DISCS!

Fireworks, 1970

Feliz Navidad, 1973

Just Wanna Rock 'n' Roll, 1975

John Fogerty.
(COURTESY OF *GUITAR PLAYER* MAGAZINE)

John Fogerty

THE FOLLOWING QUESTIONS WERE SUBMITTED
by Roger Moore of Riverhead, Long Island, New York.

What model Gibson are you presently using?

I use two Gibson Les Paul Custom guitars. One is completely unaltered, but the other has been fitted with a special 3/4"-size neck and a Bigsby tailpiece. For acoustic sound, I use a Gibson J-200.

What kind of modifications did you make on your "Acme" Rickenbacker?

Other than the "Acme" nametag, the Rickenbacker [model 425] is not modified.

What name and model of amp are you presently using?

I use a Kustom 200A-4 and a Fender Vibrolux Reverb.

Do you ever use any open tunings?

Yes. My stock Les Paul Custom is tuned down a full step, and the modified Les Paul is in standard tuning. This is done to create certain effects on some of my songs written in the key of *D*. Therefore, I switch guitars for "Proud Mary," "Bad Moon Rising," "Commotion," and a few others.

Do you hook your amps in series or parallel?

The 200- and 400-watt amps are hooked in series with a simple bridge connection from the output of the 200 to the input of the 400. Obviously, this is only used for concerts.

Is someone going to replace Tom [Fogerty]?

There are no plans to replace Tom. Creedence, I think, will continue as a trio.

Have you ever thought about making a non-Creedence-type record in the near future?

Other than a natural musical evolution, I have no plans to intentionally deviate from what I have previously created. I have no immediate plans for a solo album.

> 66 Other than a natural musical evolution, I have no plans to intentionally deviate from what I have previously created. 99

"DY-NO-MITE" DISCS!

Pendulum, Creedence Clearwater Revival, 1970

Cosmo's Factory, Creedence Clearwater Revival, 1970

John Fogerty, 1975

Peter Frampton
comes alive with
his three-pickup
Gibson Les Paul.
(COURTESY OF *GUITAR
PLAYER* MAGAZINE)

BY DON MENN

JANUARY 1974

Peter Frampton

SINCE THE AGE OF 12, PETER FRAMPTON (born April 22, 1950, in Beckenham, Kent), has been performing professionally. At 15, the British guitarist worked clubs such as the Flamingo on London's Wardour Street—the site of the birth of nearly every major British rock group from the Rolling Stones to John Mayall's Bluesbreakers. Within a year, Frampton became lead guitarist with the Herd—which produced two Top Ten singles during the time Peter toured Europe with them—before he formed the even more successful Humble Pie with Steve Marriott.

Breaking off on his own in the fall of 1971, Frampton on his *Wind of Change* proved his musical independence by playing all instruments, and was additionally backed by an impressive lineup of studio and solo stars including Billy Preston, Ringo Starr, and Klaus Voormann. As a session man himself, Peter has demonstrated his versatility in work with musicians as diverse as Rory Gallagher, Tim Hardin, Albert Lee, Alvin Lee, and Jerry Lee Lewis. Progressing from his early jazz and pop influences (ranging from Django Reinhardt and Wes Montgomery to Eddie Cochran and Cream), Peter Frampton has created a style of his own that combines both. His most recent album is *Frampton's*

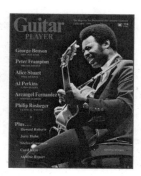

Camel, which is also the name of his most recent group.

Do you come from a musical family?

Yes. My grandmother was very musical. She used to appear playing a ukulele. My grandfather was a choir boy and into keyboards in one of the big abbeys in London. And at the time of Django Reinhardt, my father played guitar in the college dance band. He showed me the C and G chords on this ukulele I got from my grandmother when I was about seven. That was it for about a year. I didn't want to learn. But suddenly I wanted him to show me some more chords. So he got it down again.

When did you finally get your own guitar?

For Christmas, when I was eight. Four pounds ten it was—about 12 dollars. It was from an army and navy surplus store—just an ordinary steel-string guitar. It was very, very cheap, but really good for the time. I really doctored it, and got the action down low. For the following birthday, I got a pickup, and, with the help of my father, put in a volume and tone control. Then, I sold that to be able to afford my next guitar: a Hofner Club 60 Deluxe shaped like a Les Paul.

How did you amplify it?

Through our radio—one of those big old ones that had a ten-inch speaker. I've still got that one—the Hofner. I think I'm going to be using it for slide. You've got to have a guitar that has a high action, so that it doesn't buzz, and the Hofner has got the high action [*laughs*]. I'm just getting into slide. I've used it on record with Tim Hardin. It was alien to me, but I really enjoyed it. Ever since then, I've been trying to improve.

What sort of slide have you been using?

Metal, but I want to get a real glass bottleneck. I put it on my third finger, so that I can still chord.

Are you entirely self-taught?

I was, until my father asked me if I'd like to go to classical guitar when I was nine or ten. I took lessons for four years from Susan Graham in Bromley. The main thing I learned was how to use the little finger on the left hand. It amazes me that more people don't.

Do you practice now?

Only the practice I get while writing.

What were you studying at school?

Music. Harmony was the main thing. I think it was sort of to teach you how to be the conductor of an orchestra, really. I've not yet had the need for using the theory I learned, because everything is just like a jam these days—you just shout out the chords. Harmony does help when you're doing backing vocals, and knowing which chords and bass lines you can play, and when something doesn't work. But I can tell by ear, anyway. The most frustrating thing in being taught the theory of music was the fact that they used to give you a bass line, and say, "Now what we want is a tenor line, an alto line, and a soprano line on top of that." I'd sit with the guitar or the piano at home, work it out, and think, "Wow, I've got really avant-garde harmonies." I would record it, and it would sound great. But when I'd hand it in the following day, the teacher would put a red line through all of it and say, "The seventh doesn't descend—it ascends." Then, in the same breath, he'd say, "Bach does this, but Bach is the exception." I got really annoyed that Bach was allowed to do it, but I wasn't. It was frustrating.

What guitar are you using on stage now?

About four years ago, I arrived in San Francisco to do the Fillmore with Humble Pie. I had a terrible guitar. I was almost in tears trying to play it. Lo and behold, this young man called Mark Mariana came up to me and said I could borrow his black Les Paul for the next night. Believe it or not, I still have it. It's my pride and joy, and he gave it to me for nothing. Mark is a fantastic guy. I really thought things like that only happened to people you read about. The guitar has a '54 body that Mark reworked. He shaved the neck himself. It's so thin it's like custom made, and it fits my hand perfectly. He fitted a third pickup on, and put white bindings around all three. It looks amazing on stage. I think the latest pickup is a 1968. But the others must be very old, because one of them has "patent pending" written on it, and Gibson has had their patent for years. I don't think the knobs are original, but they're around 15 years old. Mark completely rewired it. I think that's the secret of the sound for me—it's out of phase. The two outside pickups are wired around the wrong way. It's wired stereo, so that if I had a stereo jack, I would have the middle pickup coming through one amp, and the outside two pickups coming through another. But I don't do that because it's too much hassle.

Are you using any other guitars now?

A Gibson Melody Maker and an Ovation 12-string—which I use for recording, but not onstage. I have a Martin acoustic that I got when I left Humble Pie. All I was doing then was sessions, and, thanks to Mark, I had the ultimate guitar for sessions. But I was also writing a lot, and it's so much nicer to write on acoustic than electric when you're not in a band. So I got a Martin D-45. The workmanship on it is just superb. I thought, "If Johnny Cash can sling one behind his back on his TV spectacular, I'll buy one and play it." It's so beautiful. It has such a full sound and beautiful sustain. It's perfectly in tune all the way up. It's the best acoustic I've ever played, and it just gets better with age. It had pure white wood when I got it. In about 18 months it'll be bright yellow. The sunlight just improves it—the wood gets more and more seasoned. When we have time enough to do our whole show, I'll be doing acoustic numbers on stage again, and then I shall use my Martin. The action is very low for an acoustic, but it doesn't buzz. On the Les Paul, it's incredibly low, too, but the pickups won't pick up the buzz.

What sort of strings do you put on?

In the jazz days, I used flatwound strings, but now I always use roundwounds—Picato ultra-light gauge. They come from Wales. On the Martin, I use D'Angelico. If I'm recording, I always change the strings for every track. When performing, I use them for two shows.

What setup are you using on stage?

I use Marshalls—two 100-watt amps through three 4x12 cabinets. So one amp uses one cabinet, and the other uses two cabinets. I have one cabinet on Mick's [Gallagher, keyboards] side, and a monitor so the others can hear me. I have two cabinets on my side of the stage. Both amps are half up. The only time I turn up flat out on the guitar is when I play a solo. With a Gibson, especially, the sound of the guitar is at its peak in tone when you've got it flat out. When you turn it down anywhere from full volume, the tone goes bassier.

I think it's cheating to use fuzz pedals, but I use a wah-wah for tone control. For recording, I use a Univibe, but they break up on stage. Then, I use a Binson Echorec. I don't use it that much for recording, because we have so many echo facilities in the studio of such high quality that there's no point. But on stage, I do like echo for a solo to lift it just that bit more. Recording, I very rarely use big amps. There's no point in playing at high volume in studios. I usually use very small amps—one of them being the Fender Champ, the smallest amp they make. You can turn it flat out, and talk above it, and it sounds like a Marshall 100-watt. That's why I like it.

What sort of pick do you use?

I use a Hofner. It's very small and very thick, and it doesn't bang at all. I hold it with my thumb and first finger just so the point sticks out. I use a new one each night. Mostly, I pick with downstrokes—except when I go fast, then it's up and down. Actually, I don't give it much thought.

What about your left-hand technique?

It's mainly a mixture of hammer-ons, pull-offs, and full barre chords. I'm a great believer in jazz chords, and I use as many as possible—thirteenths, ninths, suspended. The solos are improvised. Mostly, I get the leads off the chords.

Do you use other tunings?

On the *Wind of Change* album, I used a *D* tuning. I also use a *C* tuning that goes *E, C, G, E, C, C,* and a *G* tuning that's *G, B, D, G, B, D*.

Any advice for people just starting out?

Don't give up. Sometimes, I still feel like it when I see someone who is really good—like Leo Kottke. I'm a great fan of his. But Kottke once said to me, "If only I could use a pick." You see, there are so many styles. I know there will always be people better than me. But, then again, no one will ever play like me or like Clapton or like Django. We are all different.

What do you think you'll be doing ten years from now?

I don't think about it. But now, I'm getting into keyboards more than I have ever done before. All I'm working for at the moment is making enough money to be able to waste on my own studio. That's really what I want. One of my ambitions is to write a complete score and hand it to an orchestra. I'd love to write a film score one day—to write everything and conduct the orchestra, as well. But performing is the best thing for a musician. It keeps you from becoming stagnant. I'll never be able to stop working on the road, I'm sure. Let's face it—I'm a showoff.

"DY-NO-MITE" DISCS!

Frampton's Camel, 1973

Frampton, 1974

Frampton Comes Alive!, 1976

Robert Fripp
wrote the
popular
"Guitar Craft"
column for
Guitar Player.
(© MICHAEL
PUTLAND/
RETNA LTD.)

BY STEVE ROSEN

MAY 1974

Robert Fripp

ROBERT FRIPP, LEAD GUITARIST WITH English rock group King Crimson, is a conspicuous personality by appearing inconspicuous. Rather than stand when performing, he perches himself on a stool. The 27-year-old musician has worked in groups since he was 14, but would have given up guitaring when he was 18 to sell houses with his father, had it not been for a phone call from a hotel near his home in Bournemouth offering him a gig for $25 a week. When he was nearing 21, he decided that "becoming a professional musician would enable me to do all the things in my life that I wanted."

Fripp then formed a band that, by his description, was so bad he had to cancel gigs lest people he knew would actually come. He also backed up singers, and played in Italian restaurants, and spent a month "auditioning" for a group, which, to this day, has yet to inform him whether or not he was accepted. In 1969, he formed King Crimson with Greg Lake.

Why do you sit down on stage?

It's because you can't play guitar standing up—at least I can't. In the semi-pro bands I played in, I stood up uncomfortably. With King Crimson, I did about three or four gigs standing up, and said, "This is hopeless, I just can't play this way." Greg Lake said,

"You can't sit down—you'll look like a mushroom." I felt it wasn't my job to stand up and look moody. My job was to play, and I couldn't play standing up. I generally find it very difficult to play on stage, and I detest recording. I suppose playing live gigs is the thing I enjoy doing most. Let's put it another way: It's one of the things I dislike least.

Do you think people see you as being moody by sitting down?

I couldn't care less. The perverse thing is—from the point-of-view of stage presentation—I suppose it's given me a kind of stage presence that I wouldn't otherwise have had, because no one else does it. And that comes back to a certain thing I've always believed, which is: Just be yourself.

When did you get your first electric guitar?

When I was about 14, I bought a Hofner President and a six-watt amplifier with an eight-inch speaker. That was my first experimenting with an electric guitar.

What guitarists did you listen to?

I've never really listened to guitarists, because they've never really interested me. In fact, I think guitar is a pretty feeble instrument. Virtually nothing intrigues me about the guitar. When I was ten, I started listening to rock and roll. The first things that really got me off were the early Sun records with Scotty Moore. When I was 13, I got into trad jazz, and when I was 15, I got into modern and classical music. Just before I turned professional, I listened to some Hendrix and Clapton, and there were one or two Hendrix things I enjoyed—not the rocky things so much, but the slower things. But I haven't been influenced by Hendrix and Clapton in the way that most people would normally say it. I don't think Hendrix was a guitarist. I very much doubt if he was interested in guitar playing as such. He was just a person who had something to say, and he got on and said it. Clapton is mostly quite banal—although he did some exciting things earlier in his life with John Mayall. Mayall's *Bluesbreakers* album is superb, and Clapton does quite amazingly. I saw Cream live once. I thought they were quite awful. Clapton's work since, I think, has been excessively tedious. Jeff Beck's guitar playing I can appreciate as good fun. It's where the guitarist and "poser/ego tripper/rock star/entertainer" becomes all involved in the package. I'm not putting it down—it's good fun, quite enjoyable, and very exciting. I wish him the best of luck.

What type of guitar did you start using with King Crimson?

The Gibson Les Paul that I bought in December 1968. I started using the Les Paul, because I'd been told it was a good guitar by virtually everybody. It was the trendy thing to do then, and I thought, "Alright, I'll give it a try." Its serial number is 53—one of the early ones from the '50s. I've got two Stratocasters from about 1963 and 1966. I have a Gibson J-45 acoustic, and one of the more expensive Yamaha acoustics. I also have a Milner pre-war acoustic guitar and a pre-war Gibson tenor guitar. I disliked Fender for a long time, but I bought a couple two or three years ago in order to get into them, and, partly, as an investment. I started working with the Stratocaster this year. I liked it. It's a far better chordal guitar than the Les Paul, although I think the Les Paul is probably better for single-note work.

What types of picks and strings do you use?

I use triangular, tortoise-shell picks that are not very hard. Because my plectrum work is particularly important, it's impossible to use those very heavy plastic things. The strings I use are John Alvey Turner light gauge, but I use a medium-gauge second string for the third string. They're not what most players would consider light strings, but because most very light strings are not tempered to operate at the pitches at which they're pitched—and because I'm interested in playing chords which involve thirds or tenths—I find such tempering very difficult to accept. I usually change strings after two gigs. I used to leave them on for a week, but I found that takes the edge off things. For studio work, where that extra zing certainly helps things, I change them every two days.

What about pedals?

On stage, I use three pedals: a volume pedal, a fuzz tone, and a wah-wah. The volume pedal is by Farfisa, and it's the finest volume pedal I've found anywhere. It's the only one that goes totally off and still has a wide movement. The fuzz and wah-wah are both pretty rubbish-y. I'm not sure what type of wah-wah it is. The best fuzz box is a Burn's Buzzaround, which they discontinued making in England about six years ago. I have two of them, but they're not attached to my pedalboard at the moment. The more pedals you go through, the longer leads you need, and, in turn, the less volume you get. You lose gain along the way. To lessen that, the wah-wah and fuzz are on a knockoff circuit. In other words, I'm going through the volume pedal all the time, but the fuzz and wah-wah are run through a different circuit. So when I'm not using them, I press a button and knock them out of the circuit, and I keep up my gain. I also use a Watkins Copicat echo unit. It's all right, but it's not particularly good. It suffices for what I want, which is not really a lot of echo effects, but just a slight edge, because the sound on stage is very dead in a lot of halls I play in.

Do you feel your music has ever become a victim of all the devices?

Possibly. I mean, you tell me. I suppose if one is playing something particularly banal musically, then to make it a little more exciting, one might switch on one's wah-wah. Is that a form of escape? If it is, then, yes, I do use devices to cover up bad playing from time to time.

Why did you happen to stick with a Hiwatt amplifier?

Because it's a fairly versatile amplifier. I've had new cabinets built for me with Electro-Voice speakers in them, and I'm most impressed.

How do you hook up the guitar and amplifier?

I plug the guitar into the brilliant channel, and then plug a jump lead from the brilliant channel into normal channel. In other words, I feed the brilliant signals into the normal, and then I turn up the normal channel's gain to equal that of the brilliant channel. This adds bottom. Hiwatt has a volume control for each channel, and a master volume. If you want to have a pure sound, you turn your master up and your individual volumes down. But I turn the master volume down and both individual volumes up to get a rather hairy sound—even at a very low level.

Could you describe your picking technique?

I work on the assumption that you have two hands, so why not use each of them? I think the plectrum hand is more important than the left. I'm left-handed, incidentally, and I play the guitar right-handed. It seemed to me most people learned to play the instrument that way. When I was 15, I started developing this technique with the plectrum, whereby the ball of the thumb was pivoted on the bridge so that one picked across the strings with the ball of the thumb as a pivot. But in 1971, I started a different approach, where I lift the hand off the bridge, and operate in a kind of "free suspension" where the hand hovers above the strings. This makes crosspicking a lot easier. However, it made my playing very difficult, and it still does, because it takes three years to adopt and fully integrate a change into your playing. In five years time, it'll be a far more fluid style of playing. I'm more interested in a technique that offers a solid base for expanding. My left hand is very similar to a classical-guitar position.

Are there any scales that you usually work from?

As a basic scale, I use a diatonic major scale based on the Dorian mode. I also enjoy whole-tone scales. But it really doesn't matter—it all depends on what you're trying to create. Sometimes, the best way of evoking a certain feeling is to use a melody, and there are few things as satisfying as a superb tune, or a very nice chord change.

As a great part of Crimson's material is structured, do you have much chance for improvising?

It varies from piece to piece. But as this band isn't very sensitive or interested in listening to everyone playing, improvisation is extremely limited. It's more concerned with individuals showing off, than in developing any kind of community improvisation.

How often and do you practice?

When I first turned professional, and was unemployed, the most I did was 12 hours a day for three days running. When I came to America in 1969, I used to practice six or eight hours a day. Daily practice—and not just going through one's licks, but going through proper exercises—is most important. If your readers want to play their instrument, then they need to follow a system of training over a period of time, and practice every day. Nothing worthwhile is achieved suddenly.

It all depends on what one wants. I suggest that guitar playing can be a way of uniting the body with the personality. Working in a band is a good way of making magic. You see, I don't think of myself as a musician. Again, as I said, I think the guitar is a pretty feeble instrument. One uses the tools one has at hand, and does what one can. What affects my playing more than anything is my state of mind. I mean, obviously, there are physical things involved—like if one hasn't practiced for a week, one's muscles won't work. I've been more interested in being a musician than a guitarist. A musician creates music. A guitarist plays the guitar—which doesn't mean music is involved in it.

"DY-NO-MITE" DISCS!

No Pussyfooting, **Fripp & Eno,** 1973

Starless and Bible Black, **King Crimson,** 1974

Exposure, 1979

Jerry Garcia

JERRY GARCIA AND THE GRATEFUL DEAD HAVE BECOME cultural institutions, though they never planned it that way. Other bands have achieved a similar status, but for different reasons; unlike the major rock attractions who are idolized from afar, the Dead are

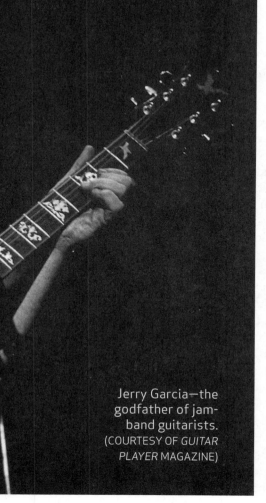

Jerry Garcia—the
godfather of jam-
band guitarists.
(COURTESY OF *GUITAR
PLAYER* MAGAZINE)

OCTOBER 1978

BY JON SIEVERT

seen up close, enjoyed, and respected. They were patriarchs of San Francisco's psychedelic colony of the 1960s, city fathers in a community of crazies. As perceived general press, Garcia and company were the hippie band, playing music for getting stoned, seeing God, dancing, singing, blowing bubbles, mellowing out, or whatever—good-time music without rock-star pretensions. But the Grateful Dead were more than that, and they have produced an extensive catalog of music that transcends the experiences of late-'60s San Francisco. Today, without hit singles, they remain heroes to their confederacy of loyal fans, or Dead Heads.

Previously, you've said that you seem to go through cyclic learning stages. What causes that to happen?

I think it's something that happens to even guitar player as he keeps on playing through the years. You're struggling to learn a whole body of material, and you finally learn it, and can play it expertly, and then you get bored. It becomes a "now what?" situation. You're struggling to obtain ground, and you reach a plateau, and then your boredom finally drives you to develop to new levels. I think that's a healthy and normal thing. I seem to go through it about once every two years

pretty regularly. I think of myself really as a guitar student as much as a player or performer, because there's so much being developed, and so much that's already been done that I'll never learn it all.

What kinds of guitars are you playing these days?

My off-and-on favorite is one that was custom-built for me by Doug Irwin. The next order of preference are the Travis Beans that I play a lot. The Ibanez people have also made me a guitar that I'm intrigued with and may use sometimes. I get stale on a guitar if I play it exclusively for a long time. Also, I've never been able to quite get what I want out of any guitar. I'm always changing it and updating it by changing pickups and things like that. I really seek a kind of universal guitar—something that will sound like anything I want it to at any given moment.

So you do use all the controls available to you on the guitar?

Yeah, whatever's there. If there were five more things I would use them, just because for me the guitar isn't really as important to me as music is. I love the guitar, and I'm trying to become a guitar player, but it's the music that counts, so the more variety I can gain, the better off I am. The other side of that is that there has to be no hassle—the guitar should be predictable and repeatable.

When did you get your Irwin guitar?

I got it around the end of 1972, and it was the first guitar that Doug built with his name on it. He used to work for Alembic. We worked together on the design, and it has been through a constant transformation process since—we just installed DiMarzio pickups, for example. The guitar body is western maple with a core of purpleheart wood [amaranth], which is very hard. The wolf inlay was originally a decal that I put on when I got the guitar. I sent it to Doug for some kind of work, and when it came back he had duplicated the decal exactly with inlays.

What's the purpose of the two jacks on the front of the Irwin guitar?

That's the one real wiring innovation—a very useful one. It allows me to have all my effects pedals wired to the guitar with the ability to bypass them all with a switch. I use a stereo cord, and the signal goes from the pickups to the tone controls and pickup switch, and on down the "A" side of the cord to a network box that controls a Mu-Tron octave divider, Mu-Tron envelope filter, MXR Distortion Plus, MXR phaser, Mu-Tron wah-wah, and an analog delay. The signal goes through the devices, back into the network box, and up the "B" side of the cord, back into the instrument before the volume pot, and then out to the amp.

What's the advantage to this setup?

All of those gadgets are voltage-sensitive. If you have them after the volume control, their behavior is affected by the loudness setting on the guitar. With my system, on the other hand, the effects always see the guitar as if it had full output voltage. The effects are also controlled by a DC power supply, rather than batteries. Because the effects' input voltage is always fixed, they behave exactly the way I want them to. The whole thing is so stable

❝ I am very attracted to melody. ❞

that it's completely repeatable in every situation. I'd used effects in recording before, but they were always too unstable for me to use onstage until we came up with this. If something goes wrong with the effects, or if I want them out of the circuit, all I have to do is flip a switch to completely bypass them without a jump or loss in gain at the amp.

Could you discuss your approach to fingering?

I think it has something to do with my early five-string banjo playing. Most guitar players I've noticed seem to use a flat fingering. I've somehow trained myself to come straight down on top of the string. I play mostly on the tips of my fingers, so the high action doesn't get in my way at all. I'm not pulling other strings along with it and so forth.

Do you use the little finger on your left hand much?

Yes. Early on, I was lucky enough to have someone point out the usefulness of that finger. As a result it is one of my stronger fingers, and I prefer to use it even more than my ring finger. That's always made me different from most rock guitarists that] know—even the really good ones. I think in rock and roll a lot of guitar players favor something that lets them use the ring finger for greater articulation and vibrato effects. For me, I've got to be able to do it with every finger. I find it ridiculous to have to close all my ideas on my ring finger just so I can get a vibrato. That eliminates a lot of possibilities automatically.

How do you achieve your vibrato?

Well, I have about four or five different families of vibrato. Some of them are unsupported—nothing is touching the guitar but my finger on the string. Other methods are supported, and I just move the finger for the sound. Sometimes, I also use wrist motion, and other times I'll move my whole arm. I also use horizontal and lateral motion for different sound and speed. Each has its own separate sound, and it depends on what I'm going after and which finger I'm leading with. For example, if you're playing the blues, it's generally appropriate to use a slow vibrato. Generally speaking, I tend to be style-conscious in terms of wanting a song to sound like the world it comes from.

Do you play many notes by hammering on and pulling off?

Generally, I like to pick every note, but I do tend to pull off, say, a real fast triplet on things that are closing up-intervals that are heading up the scale. I do it almost without thinking about it. I almost never pull off just one note. I seldom hammer on, because it seems to have a certain inexactitude for me. I think that was a decision I made while playing the banjo. My preference is for the well-spoken tone, and I think coming straight down on the strings with high knuckles makes it. So my little groups of pull-offs are really well articulated—it's something I worked on a lot.

How do you approach right-hand technique?

Generally, I use a Fender extra heavy flatpick, which I sometimes palm when using my fingers. The way I hold the pick is a bit strange, I guess. I don't hold it in the standard way but more like you hold a pencil. I think Howard Roberts describes it as the scalpel technique. The motion is basically generated from the thumb and first finger rather than say, the wrist or elbow. But I use all different kinds of motion, depending on whether I am doing single-string stuff or chords.

Do you find your middle-finger injury causing any problems?

Not at all. My brother cut it off with an axe when I was four years old, so I've been without it for a long time. Actually, it might have even helped me because of the independence I've developed. Normally your first two fingers and your last two fingers tend to work as units. I used the first and ring fingers to develop my three-finger banjo style, so I have total independence in the fingers. Also, I can tuck the pick between the first finger and the stub and easily switch to fingerpicking.

Could you discuss your distinctive approach to accenting?

Again, a certain amount of it is related to banjo playing, where you have problem solving continually going on. There are three fingers moving more or less constantly, and you have to change the melodic weight from anyone finger to any other finger. What that really involves is rhythmic changes. So for me it's always been interesting to have little surprises like, for instance, accenting all the *off*-beats for a bar. There's also the constant playing in odd times with the Grateful

Dead that contributes to that. For instance, if the band is playing in 7/4 time, I might play in 4/4. When you do that sort of thing, you begin to notice certain ways in which the two rhythms synchronize over a long period of time. Thinking in these long lengths, you automatically start to develop rhythmic ideas that have a way of interconnecting. If you're in the right kind of rhythmic context, then you have the option of being able to continually reevaluate your position in time. For me it then becomes a thing of syncopations based on other syncopations. For example, I like to start an idea when the music is in flow on a 16th-note triplet off of four. So that's like intensely syncopated on its own, and if I start my phrase there, it's like constructing one sentence off of another one before the first sentence is completed. That sort of linguistic analogy is something I'm very attracted to.

What process do you go through for building solos?

The way I start is to learn the literal melody of the tune—if there is one. Then I construct solos as though that were happening, and I'm either playing with it or against it. That's a pretty loose description, obviously, because there are a lot of other factors involved. Later on, I start to see other kinds of connections, but one of my first processes is to learn the literal melody in any position. I am very attracted to melody. A song with a beautiful melody can just knock me off my feet, but the greatest changes on earth don't mean anything to me if they don't have a great melody tying them together in some sense.

Could you say a few words about any merits or disadvantages of playing stoned?

There's a thing about playing stoned without having pressure on you to play com-

"DY-NO-MITE" DISCS!

Workingman's Dead, Grateful Dead, 1970

American Beauty, Grateful Dead, 1970

Europe '72, Grateful Dead, 1972

petently. If you have the space in your life where you can be high and play and not be in a critical situation, you can learn a lot of interesting things about yourself and your relation to the instrument and music. We were lucky enough to have an uncritical situation, so it wasn't like a test of how stoned we could be and still be competent—we weren't concerned with being competent. We were more concerned with being high at the time. The biggest single problem from a practical point of view is that obviously your perception of time gets all weird. Now, that can be interesting, but from a practical standpoint, I try to avoid extremes of any sort, because you have the fundamental problems of playing in tune and playing with everybody else. People have to pay a lot of money to see us, so it becomes a matter of professionalism. You don't want to deliver somebody a clunker just because you're too high.

David Gilmour's soaring guitar leads were a thrilling element of Pink Floyd's sound. (JORGEN ANGEL/RETNA LTD.)

BY STEVE ROSEN

MAY 1979

David Gilmour

DAVID GILMOUR HAS BEEN PLAYING GUITAR
with Pink Floyd for 11 years now—about one-third
of his life. And, for more than a decade, his style has
been undergoing a constant refining process that parallels the band's evolution from a spearhead of the psychedelic movement of the 1960s, to a mainstay of the outer-
space rock of the 1970s.

Joining Pink Floyd in February 1968—after the
band's original guitarist and founder, Syd Barrett, began
to show wear and tear from drugs and the band's almost
constant touring—Gilmour was relegated to rhythm guitar. In early April of the same year, Barrett left the band,
and Gilmour, then 21 years old, became the group's only
guitarist. He proceeded to carry on with the chores of
upholding the band's tradition of psychedelia that had
made them standouts on the British music scene.

With Barrett at the helm, Pink Floyd had released
one album, *The Piper at the Gates of Dawn*, and had
achieved fame in England for their
innovative use of light shows. The
band had already established a
momentum when Gilmour joined,
and, at the end of June 1968, their
second album, *A Saucerful of Secrets*,
was released. Since that album, the
personnel of Pink Floyd has remained

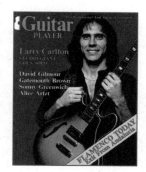

static, with Gilmour, keyboardist Rick Wright, bassist Roger Waters, and drummer Nick Mason. As a unit, they expanded their musical abilities, and consistently drew critical praise for their use of quadraphonic sound and visual special effects.

In October 1970, *Atom Heart Mother*, was released, and propelling the LP was the addition of a horn section and male and female choruses. This fourth album reached number one on the British charts, and it was followed in 1971 by the less well-received *Meddle*. The group spent the majority of 1972 recording what was to be their tour de force: *Dark Side of the Moon*. This 1973 release became Pink Floyd's first number-one album in the United States, and was a mainstay on the British charts for two years. The band toured throughout 1973, and then went into a period of semi-retirement that lasted until the release of *Wish You Were Here* in 1975, which was followed by *Animals* in 1977.

In 1978, Gilmour was the first member of Pink Floyd to release a solo album, simply entitled *David Gilmour*. While there are obvious parallels between Gilmour's solo work and his efforts with Pink Floyd, the album stands on its own, and shows that David has long passed the stage of being a replacement for another musician. He is an identifiable guitarist with his own distinct style that lends instant recognition to anything he does.

Born in Cambridge, England, on March 6, 1947, Gilmour began playing when he was 14 years old, on a nylon-string Spanish guitar lent to him by his next-door neighbor. His main instruction came from playing along with records until his parents bought him a Pete Seeger tutoring album. Young Gilmour was always acutely aware of the popular music scene, and was interested primarily in the folk and rock and roll genres. He listened to everyone from Seeger to Bill Haley, and after playing on his own for a couple of years, he started to become involved with his first bands. It was then that he bought another acoustic guitar—with f-holes—and planted an electric pickup in it. Upon feeling the power of an electric guitar, he was hooked. Soon, he acquired a Burns Sonnet, which he says was dreadful. He used it for a short time until he switched to a Hofner Club 60.

David used the Hofner until his parents surprised him by giving him a Fender Telecaster—which they had bought on a trip to the United States, where Fenders were far less expensive than they were in England—for his 21st birthday. The Telecaster remained with Gilmour for one year, until he made his first flight to the United States, where it was lost by one of the airlines.

For the first few months of his Pink Floyd tenure, Gilmour assumed the role of rhythm guitarist alongside Barrett.

"I was playing rhythm guitar, and Syd wasn't really playing anything," says David about Syd's growing disorientation in the band. "I didn't really start playing lead guitar for a long time. I didn't know what to do. I was a bit lost for quite a while, so I just stuck to the chords, and sang to words on the record—which is what they wanted at the time in order to fulfill their contractual obligations. It took me some time to actually feel my way around, and become completely assimilated."

A Saucerful of Secrets marked Gilmour's first appearance on record. David was still feeling around in the dark on this release, and while he performed several solos on it, he states there is nothing that he found particularly profound in his work. For this album, he was using a Selmer 50-watt amplifier with a single cabinet containing four 12" speakers, and a Binson echo unit. His guitar was a second Telecaster that he had purchased. This was later stolen, and David replaced it with a Stratocaster. Eventually, the Selmer amp was replaced with Hiwatt gear, and effects pedals started creeping into his setup.

"I worked up to where I had a huge line of them all sitting onstage with wires everywhere," says Gilmour. "But batteries kept running out, and everything kept breaking. Eventually, I had to consolidate them."

In 1972, all the pedals were built into a special cabinet—although, since then, he has gone through several different setups. Gilmour's current stage panel consists of an MXR Phase 90, an Electro-Harmonix Electric Mistress, an Orange treble and bass booster, a Big Muff, an Arbiter Fuzz Face, and a custom-built tone pedal. All pedals are wired so that any one of them can be bypassed. Other effects can be incorporated into the system, and there are three outputs that allow David to simultaneously route signals to different amplifiers.

David currently uses three Stratocasters, two Telecasters, and a Gibson Les Paul. His main guitar is a black 1979 Stratocaster with a DiMarzio pickup and a 1962 neck. The fretboard is rosewood, although Gilmour generally prefers the sound and feel of maple boards. The Stratocaster has also been fitted with an extra switch that allows him to add the neck pickup in any combination with the other pickups. Another guitar he frequently uses is a 1955 Fender Esquire with a neck pickup added by Seymour Duncan.

"I never got on with Gibsons," he says of his decision to stick almost exclusively to Fender guitars. "I think people tend to stick with what they started off with. When I was a lad, I always wanted a Fender because the people I saw and dug were playing Fenders."

Hiwatt amplifiers have been with David since the early days. He uses two 100-watt stacks, and two 200-watt Yamaha rotary speaker systems. All of his cabinets are made by WEM. In the studio, he will often go for a Fender Twin Reverb or a Mesa/Boogie.

Gilmour also dabbles with acoustic guitar, and he owns two Martins—a D-18 and a D-35. He occasionally plays acoustic onstage, and he alternates between fingerpicking and using a plectrum.

David always uses a Herco heavy-gauge pick on electric. He started out using Gibson Sonomatic strings, but found them a bit too heavy, and changed to lighter sets of Ernie Balls. He now uses Sonomatics again, but in custom gauges. His studio setup is .010, .012, .016, .024, .034, and .044. His live-performance gauges are .010, .012, .016, .028, .038, and .050.

Gilmour admits he is a bit heavy-handed in his playing approach, but makes it clear that it is a major factor in his style. His lead work does not often involve fast lines, but rather melodic and moving phrases.

"I've never managed to become a very light-fingered guitarist," he says. "I'm not that sort of player. I don't really mind that, though. I'd like to have the technique there, but I think a lot of other people abuse it."

For Gilmour to work up a solo in the studio, he will usually play around the neck, paying little attention to the key of the song or where his fingers fall. He tries to poke around in the dark, hoping that something unusual will crop up. Once he finds a spark, he develops and shapes it into a full form. When he feels confident that the solo is ready to record, he will tape it after just one or two run-throughs. At times, David will use a simple hammer-on/off technique to add speed to his runs.

"I try to sound faster than I am," he says. "For just a few seconds, a tiny bit of sheer speed is very effective if it's put into a proper context. Basically, I'm a person who is stuck within certain limitations, and I have to work within them."

Gilmour is very pleased with the guitar work on his solo album. He feels he approached the instrument in much the same fashion he does with Pink Floyd, but thinks the solos are a bit more "off the cuff' and fresher. And while it is often rumored that Gilmour dabbles in all manners of studio wizardry, he in fact does very little. He employs both close and far miking to achieve dimension in the sound, and will lay down rhythm tracks first, and then overdub leads and vocals. He views the production of a good guitar sound as a permanent struggle. He looks for a bright tone, but one that embodies some low end, as well.

A major part of Gilmour's sound revolves around his use of a vibrato bar, which was one of the main reasons for his playing a Stratocaster. Because he has used the vibrato for years, he has found that certain adjustments aid in keeping the guitar from going out of tune. In front of the vibrato unit are six screws that fit directly into the top of the guitar body from above. If these are the least bit loose, the main block of the unit will move up and down, causing the guitar to go out of tune. To eliminate the problem, Gilmour removes the strings from the guitar, and tightens each of the six screws so that they touch the surface of the plate. As there is no gap between the screws and the plate, there is no room for movement. Gilmour switches from three to four springs in the vibrato tailpiece depending on the situation. Onstage, he uses four springs, and goes for three in the studio.

While Gilmour has gone through periods of intense practice to see whether he could bring more speed to his playing, he has found that there has been no dramatic change in his technique. However, he does feel that his playing on *David Gilmour* is as creative as anything he has ever produced.

"I think my playing is as strong as it has ever been," he says. "There have been periods when I was very in practice— such as when we had been working on the road for a long time. Generally speaking, I feel I'm playing as well as I can, but I still think I can improve."

"DY-NO-MITE" DISCS!

Meddle, **Pink Floyd,** 1971

The Dark Side of the Moon, **Pink Floyd,** 1973

Wish You Were Here, **Pink Floyd,** 1975

Steve Hackett
helped pioneer
prog-rock guitar
with Genesis in
the '70s.
(COURTESY OF
GUITAR PLAYER
MAGAZINE)

Steve Hackett

STEVE HACKETT IS THE CREATIVE LEAD GUITARIST *for the British band Genesis. The following questions were submitted by John Simon of Boulder, Colorado.*

Who were some of your early influences on the guitar?

Oh, Cliff Richards and the Shadows, Jeff Beck, and Peter Green.

How long have you been playing guitar?

About ten years.

Did you have any overall guiding perspective to playing guitar?

No, I didn't. You see, what I tried to do when I first started was to play in a certain style, but that didn't satisfy me. I found I liked listening just as much to Segovia as I liked listening to Hendrix. And with Genesis, it has always been our policy to play from as wide a base as possible. For me, I'm happier being able to sketch in a number of different types of music, than to be in any one particular musical field.

What is your view on special-effects devices?

I think they just broaden the scope of what an instrument is capable of doing. The problem is, at the moment, that the electric guitar is an adaptation of an instrument which has already been—the acoustic guitar.

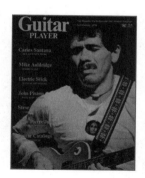

What I'm after is an elec*tronic* guitar—not an electric guitar. But special effect devices are just a means to an end. Like, I don't have any more reverence for a 1952 Les Paul than I do for a 1974 fuzz box. They are all just part of music. The guitar is of lesser importance to me than my range of effects. The sound is everything—getting the right tone.

> ❝ For me, I'm happier being able to sketch in a number of different types of music, than to be in any one particular musical field. ❞

What kind of guitar do you use?

A new Gibson Les Paul.

What special effects devices do you use?

I have an octave divider, a Marshall Super Fuzz and a Duo-Fuzz, a Cry Baby wah-wah, a Schaller volume pedal, an Electro-Harmonix phasing unit, an Echoplex, and a H&H transistor amplifier with reverb, tremolo, and a distortion boost.

What kind of strings and pick do you use?

Sound City 4000—a .010 set. My pick is a Fender Medium.

Have you ever studied music?

No. I just listened to things.

Was there any point where you felt your guitar playing was finally good enough to be put onstage?

Well, I think every guitarist goes through periods of supreme confidence, and supreme lack of confidence. Some days go very well, and others not so well. And I've always been like that. Finally, I had to be more practical about

"DY-NO-MITE" DISCS!

Foxtrot,
Genesis, 1972

Voyage of the
Acolyte, 1975

Please Don't
Touch!, 1978

it. You have to see the thing for what it is, and become consistent in your playing—which comes with earning a living at it. The first time I got on a stage with a band, I was scared to death, and I just died. It was a horrible experience. The second gig I did, I went on shaking, white, and scared, but the crowd dug it, so it gave me confidence.

Jimi Hendrix.
(COURTESY OF
GUITAR PLAYER
MAGAZINE)

Jimi Hendrix

FEBRUARY 4, 1970—A DAY SO COLD AND SNOWY
that all the cabs in New York were occupied, John Burks
(then managing editor of Rolling Stone), shivering in his
California clothes, trudged and skidded through frozen slush to
a chic midtown apartment to conduct what proved to be one of
Jimi Hendrix's last major interviews.

In attendance were Jimi, Noel Redding, Mitch Mitchell,
various management personnel, and Baron Wolman, the well-
known photographer/journalist. The meeting had been initiated
by Hendrix's management primarily to trumpet the reunifica-
tion of the original Jimi Hendrix Experience, which turned out
to be a short-lived regrouping that ran concurrently with the
Band of Gypsys.

Unfortunately, the interview tape itself—a hissy jumble of
voices interrupting voices captured by a wobbly recorder—was
so discouraging in quality that Burks snatched from it what he
could for a quick article, and stashed it away in a box where it
rested untranscribed, but fortunately not erased, for the last half
decade. Though it does not always dwell
on areas normally covered by Guitar
Player, this interview nevertheless provides a last intriguing glimpse of a guitar
genius.—Don Menn, Editor

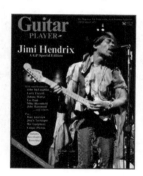

**When you put together a song,
does it just come to you, or is it a
process where you sit down with
your guitar?**

The music I might hear, I can't get on the guitar. It's a thing of just laying around daydreaming or something. You're hearing all this music, and you just can't get it on the guitar. As a matter of fact, if you pick up your guitar and just try to play, it spoils the whole thing. I can't play the guitar that well to get all this music together, so I just lay around. I wish I could have learned how to write for instruments. I'm going to get into that next, I guess.

So, for something like "Foxey Lady," you first hear the music, and then arrive at the words for the song?

It all depends. On "Foxey Lady," we just started playing, and we set up a microphone, and I had these words. With "Voodoo Child (Slight Return)," somebody was filming when we started doing that. We did that about three times because they wanted to film us in the studio— [*imitates a pompous voice*] "Make it look like you're recording, boys!" One of them scenes, you know. So, it was, "Okay, let's play this in *E*. Now a-one and-a-two and-a-three," and then we went into "Voodoo Child."

When I hear Mitch churning away and you really blowing on top and the bass getting really free, the whole approach almost sounds like avant-garde jazz.

Well, that's because that's where it's coming from—the drumming.

Do you dig any avant-garde jazz players?

Yeah. We went to Sweden, and we heard some of those cats we'd never heard before. These cats were actually in little country clubs and little caves blowing some sounds that, you know, you barely imagine. Guys from Sweden, Copenhagen, Amsterdam, and Stockholm. Every once in a while, they start going like a wave. They get into each other every once in a while within their personalities, and the party last night, or the hangover [*laughs*], and the evil starts pulling them away again. You can hear it start to go away. Then it starts getting together again. It's like a wave, I guess, coming in and out.

For your own musical kicks, where's the best place to play?

I like after-hour jams at a small club. Then you get another feeling. You get off in another way with all those people there. You get another feeling, and you mix it in with something else that you get. It's not the spotlights—it's just the people.

How are those two experiences different?

I get more of a dreamy thing from the audience. It's more of a thing that you go up into. You get into such a pitch sometimes that you forget about the audience, but you also forget about all the paranoia—that thing where you're saying, "Oh, gosh, I'm onstage—what am I going to do now?" Then you go into this other thing, and it turns out to be almost like a play in certain ways.

How much of a part do you play in the production of your albums? For example, did you produce *Are You Experienced*?

No, it was Chas Chandler and Eddie Kramer who mostly worked on that stuff. Eddie was the engineer, and Chas, as producer, mainly kept things together.

You were listed as the producer of *Electric Ladyland* . . .

All I did was just be there and make sure the right songs were there, and the sound was there. We wanted a particular

> **"I like electric sounds, feedback, static, and so forth. "**

sound. It got lost in the cutting room, because we went on tour right before we finished. I heard it, and I think the sound of it is very cloudy.

Which musicians do you go out of your way to hear?

Nina Simone and Mountain. I dig them.

What about a group like the McCoys?

Yeah, that guitar player is great. [*Sings intro to "Hang On Sloopy," which featured Rick Derringer on guitar.*]

Do you dig parodies like the Masked Marauders or the English radio program, *The Goon Show*?

I never heard it. I heard about it. The Fugs—they're good. I've heard they don't have *The Goon Show* over here. They're the funniest things I've ever heard—besides Pinky Lee. Remember Pinky Lee? They were like a classic of a whole lot of Pinky Lees put together, and just flip them out together.

You were a Pinky Lee fan?

I used to be. I used to wear white socks.

Were you really rehearsing with Band of Gypsys 12 to 18 hours a day?

We used to go and jam, actually. We'd say, "rehearsing" just to make it sound, you know, official. We were just getting off, that's all. Not really 18 hours—say about 12 or 14, maybe [*laughs*]. The longest the Experience ever played together is going onstage. We played about two-and-a-half hours—almost three hours one time. We made sounds. People make sounds when they clap. So we make sounds back. I like electric sounds, feedback, static, and so forth.

Are you going to do a single, as well as an LP?

All these record companies, they want singles. But you don't just sit there and say, "Let's make a track. Let's make a single or something." We don't do that.

Creedence Clearwater Revival does that until they have enough for a record, like in the old days.

Well, that's the old days. I consider us more musicians—more in the minds of musicians, you know?

But singles can make some bread, can't they?

Well, that's why they do them. But they take it after. You'll have a whole planned out LP, and all of a sudden they'll make, for instance, "Crosstown Traffic" a single, and that's coming out of nowhere. See, that LP was in certain ways of thinking—the sides were played in order for certain reasons. And then it's almost like a sin for them to take out something in the middle of all that, make it a single, and represent us at that particular time because they think they can make more money. They always take out the wrong ones.

Ever think about getting other guitar players into your trip?

Oh, yeah. I heard Duane Eddy came into town this morning [*laughs*]. He was groovy.

Have you jammed with Larry Coryell, Sonny Sharrock, and people like that?

"DY-NO-MITE" DISCS!

Electric Ladyland, 1968

Band of Gypsys, 1970

Larry and I had like swift jams down at the Scene. Every once in a while, we would finally get a chance to get together. But I haven't had a chance to really play with him—not lately, anyway. I sort of miss that.

Do you listen to them?

I like Larry Coryell.

Better than others?

Oh, not better. Who's the other guy? I think I've heard some of his things.

Sonny Sharrock? He's all over the guitar. Sometimes, it sounds like it's not too orderly.

Sounds like someone we know, huh [*laughs*]?

Have you played with people like Roland Kirk?

Oh yeah, I had a jam with him at Ronnie Scott's in London, and I really got off. It was great. It was really great. I was so scared! It's really funny—I mean Roland, that cat gets all those sounds. I might just hit one note, and it might be interfering, but we got along great, I thought. He told me I should have turned it up or something.

Do you listen to the Band?

It's there. They got their own thing together that takes you to a certain place—takes you where they want to go [*laughs*]. They play their things onstage exactly how they play it on record.

Have movie people tried to lure you into films by saying you'd be a hell of a gunslinger or an astronaut?

An astronaut! No, well, you know—I'm trying to get the guitar together really.

Do you find American audiences more violent than those of other countries?

In New York, it's more of a violent climate. It's very violent, actually. They don't know it, really. But Texas is really fine. I don't know why—maybe it's the weather, and the feeling of it. I dig the South a little more than playing in the North. It's more of a pressure playing in the Midwest—like Cleveland or Chicago. It's like being in a blow off. The people there are groovy, but it's just the atmosphere or something, you know? But the South is great. New Orleans is great. Arizona is great. Utah.

How did they treat you in Utah?

Well, once we're off stage, it's another world, but the people are great. But when we play at the gigs, they were really listening. They were really tuned in some kind of way or another. I think it was the air.

Your tastes seem broader than the typical rock and roll fan.

This is all I can play when I'm playing. I'd like to get something together—like with Handel, Bach, and Muddy Waters. A flamenco type of thing [*laughs*]. If I could get that sound, I'd be happy.

Steve Howe rocked
Yes with classical gui-
tars and a jazz-pedi-
greed Gibson ES-175.
(COURTESY OF *GUITAR
PLAYER* MAGAZINE)

BY MICHAEL BROOKS

APRIL 1973

Steve Howe

WHEN YES FINISHED ITS SET AT BILL
Graham's Winterland in San Francisco, there was
little doubt as to the seriousness with which this five-
man English jazz/rock group approached its music. In
the words of lead guitarist, Steve Howe, "We don't wiggle our bottoms too much, and we don't grin much. This
has put some people off, but by the end of the set, I think
most are convinced of our convictions."

And it is precisely those convictions which have given
Yes its protrusion from the ordinary. The band offers a
tight, well-rehearsed, and tastefully but sparingly improvised performance. In its musical compositions, Yes is
quite free, but in performance that freedom isn't exploit-
ed to the point of meaningless and never-ending solos.

**When did you first realize you had musical aspira-
tions?**

I think I was about ten years old when I first knew
that I liked music, and I was kind of dancing around to
march records. My parents had a
weird collection of records that con-
sisted of Mantovani and Lawrence
Welk kinds of things, but dance-band
music, as well. They had all the Les
Paul and Mary Ford records, too.
Then, suddenly I got the razzle-dazzle
music with Bill Haley. I heard his

record and all those guitars playing, so I bought it. Franny Beecher, the guitarist with Haley, was really quite exceptional. So, within a couple of years, I decided I wanted to play and my parents bought me a guitar.

Did you begin with lessons?

No, and, in fact, my parents were quite happy that I got along by myself. By 12, when I had my guitar, rock and roll was really doing something to me, and I felt like part of that whole movement.

> 66 In my case, I get inspiration from every kind of music, so I was always trying to develop a style that incorporated bits of *all* the styles. 99

There were no other music forms you liked, other than rock and roll?

Well, I had an older brother and his musical tastes just slipped by rock and roll. He liked jazz, and he decided to move on to classical, and I had kind of a time lag of realizing music my brother was getting into. He took up clarinet, but with two instruments in the house it was chaotic, so with my parents' suggestion, he quit. Then, his tastes swayed, and he started listening to Chico Hamilton and some modern jazz. Anyway, he bought me Barney Kessel's *The Poll Winners* album, and told me to stop listening to Bill Haley. I thought that album was completely fantastic. I just loved it.

It would seem that you also had some early classical influences?

By 18, I had gone through the whole corridor of music—from rock to jazz to classical—and I started realizing that I could sit down and listen to classical music without it kind of imposing on me. Most people think that classical music is much too heavy, and yet it isn't. There's some light classical music in concertos and such that is just moving music—daydreaming material.

Did you ever view these diverse influences as a drawback to specialization?

Absolutely. I like every kind of music, and this held me back for a long time, because I kept verging off in different directions. But I've always played a variety of styles on the guitar. I've never played strictly blues or strictly jazz, and my technique has never pushed me into any one kind of hole. It has been more like a garden, where I pick roses here and there. I might sit down and learn a bit of classical guitar, but, six months later, I may be working out a Chuck Berry solo for the fun of it. I'm completely fascinated by the guitar as an instrument.

Who were some of your early guitar influences?

Quite an early influence was a guitarist named Les Spann—even though he didn't make it in the polls or anything. Other influences would be Les Paul and Mary Ford—which, by the way, I still listen to today. I listen to the same records I was listening to when I was ten, and they still maintain an aura about them. But in the beginning, it was rock and roll.

Like Cliff Richard and the Shadows?

Well, sure. The Shadows came on quite heavily in England with "Apache" and all that. They really sound quite dreadful now, but, at the time, I liked them very much and used to work out their tunes.

Who else?

Chet Atkins was a tremendous influence on me, and Charlie Christian always stands out. But, at home, I mainly listen to Julian Bream. I find that in listening to Charlie Christian, he isn't as much a perfectionist as Bream, and I like perfection if it has still got the feeling of the music. So there might be parts in Les Paul, Chet Atkins, Charlie Byrd, or Tal Farlow records that I don't like. But the ultimate thing with Julian Bream is that I like everything he does as soon as the record starts.

How does the Bream influence—along with all the other influences—fit into Yes? Are they all compatible?

Well, there is a great mass of influences. I mean, in Yes we somehow have to fit everything in. Lately, we've been talking an awful lot about ourselves, and we've never done that before. We've never stopped and asked what Yes is really doing. In England, somebody once said, "Yes play music, and the things they play together are things people don't normally play together."

Initially, I imagine you arrive as quite a shock to your audiences—especially as your music is not easy to categorize.

I don't think that, at first, America was quite ready for us—a group that came on and didn't wiggle its bottoms too much, and didn't grin very much. This has put some people off, but, by the end of our set, I think most are convinced of our convictions. We are dedicated, and we would still be playing even if we were stuck living in broken-down surroundings. We've all been through not having anything to hang onto except our music.

How did you begin developing your lead style?

I've always found it difficult to sit down and work licks off records. About three years after I started playing, I used to sit down with a Kenny Burrell or Django Reinhardt solo. I'd have to slow the phonograph down to 16 rpm, but the guitars still seemed just as fast. So, I used to work out a few top lines—maybe just a chorus—and play them a couple of times to find out why I was playing everything wrong. But I didn't get too discouraged, because I think if you can interpret a few things wrong, it's good. You see, the act of not getting it quite right, and then adding a certain amount of your own personality to the licks, is what can start you developing your own style. In my case, I get inspiration from every kind of music, so I was always trying to develop a style that incorporated bits of *all* the styles.

In your guitar playing, is it a conscious thought to steer away from contemporary lead licks and such that are obvious?

I don't know whether I'm about 20 years behind, or 20 years ahead, but I find that I'm not prepared to play the general style of today's guitar. I've basically never liked "in-vogue" guitar playing. It always seems you hear too much of it. So I really try to avoid the ordinary licks. If somebody presents me with an A chord, I can flash on the A position, but I'll also think about the relative minor and the relative minor seventh against the A, and I'll try to do away with the root note. I always try to steer away from the obvious.

Have you modified your Gibson ES-175?

Well, I put Grover tuning machines on that, and a new bridge. I've turned the treble [bridge] pickup around—which is a bit of a secret that

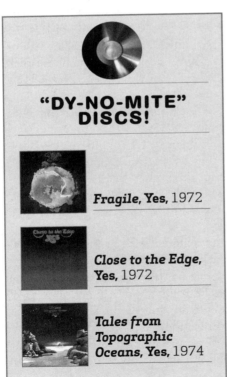

"DY-NO-MITE" DISCS!

Fragile, Yes, 1972

Close to the Edge, Yes, 1972

Tales from Topographic Oceans, Yes, 1974

has helped me get a slightly different sound. By turning it around, the polepieces are about an inch further from where they would normally be. This diminishes the sharp, "rear guard" sound you tend to get right at the back of the bridge, so you get more warmth—a little bit more tone and a little less treble.

What amplifier are you using?

It's a Fender Dual Showman with two Dual Showman cabinets. My amp settings are very basic—volume is at seven—and the tone control on the guitar is at ten, and the guitar's volume control is at ten, as well. I'll sometimes dial the guitar's volume down to eight. I don't use the tone controls on the guitar very often.

What about strings and picks?

On my Martin acoustic, I use light-gauge Martin strings. On the Gibson, I use medium-gauge Gibson Sonomatics, but I use two firsts, then a second, a third, and then the fifth and sixth strings straight [.012, .012, .015, .028, .044, .056]. I change strings every night when on the road.

I've got a very odd pick. It's Plexiglas. An old man makes them, and they're about 1/8" to 3/16" thick, tapering down to a sharp edge at the playing point. Because of the pick's size, it seems bulky, but in that you have control. Thin plectrums bend too much, and give you a different sound.

What's on your pedalboard?

I've got a line of four switches on top of the board that control a sound-on-sound device, an Echoplex, a reverb, and a tremolo. The rest of the board consists of a Marshall Fuzz box, a Cry Baby wah-wah, a Fender volume pedal, a Maestro fuzz tone, and a ring modulator.

On an ending note, I realize you must have a great deal of respect for classical artists, but did you ever notice how they are secondary to the music, whereas in rock it's the other way around?

I know just what you mean. It's important to the rock audience to know who is playing the music—whether it's George Harrison, or somebody doing Harrison's music. If it's by the name, you might buy it, but if it's somebody else doing the music, you probably wouldn't. The people playing classical music always seem to take a second best, because the music is the important thing.

Black Sabbath's prince of
the dark riff—Tony Iommi.
(CHRIS WALTER/WIREIMAGE/
GETTY IMAGES)

BY STEVE ROSEN

OCTOBER 1974

Tony Iommi

BLACK SABBATH LEAD GUITARIST TONY IOMMI stands well over six-feet tall, and plays like he has six fingers. Not bad, since several years ago, Tony hacked off the ends of his middle and ring fingers on his right hand (he plays left-handed), and consequently had to completely alter his playing. Struggling with various types of plastic tips which he has placed at the ends of the fingers, he has since gone on to become one of the more stylistic players on the rock scene today.

Tony always had an interest in music, though. His first aspiration was to be a drummer, but owing to lack of funds, he turned to a less expensive instrument. The guitar came in almost by default.

"I got a guitar for a birthday present," he states, "and things just went on from there."

His first substantial electric guitar was a Watkins, which ran through a small Watkins tube amplifier. During these early years of his playing, Tony would frequently get together with friends and jam, but nothing ever came about until he auditioned with Jethro Tull, and scored the lead-guitarist position. This was in 1969, following Mick Abrahams's departure, and preceding the band's appearance in the Rolling Stones' *Rock 'n' Roll Circus*

film. Tony was with Tull for the filming of the show only, and immediately left the band after the project was finished.

"It just wasn't right, so I left," he explains. "At first, I thought the band was great, but I didn't much go for having a leader in the band—which was Ian Anderson's way—and the communication between band members wasn't too friendly. As we are now in Black Sabbath, there is no leader. Everyone does their own part."

Originally, Iommi had left Sabbath to join Tull, but swiftly returned to his former band. His first guitar with Sabbath was a Fender Stratocaster. As the band grew in popularity, they were offered an attractive advertising arrangement by Laney amplifiers. Since that time, Tony has been using six 4x12 Laney cabinets that are fed by four, 100-watt Laney amps.

After using the Fender for several years, Iommi changed to Gibson, and he now uses an SG. One major alteration has been the replacement of the pickups with specially built low-feedback units. Tony thought the standard Gibson pickups fed back uncontrollably, and—though the sound they produced was more than satisfactory—the searing screeches that accompanied that sound made the pickups impossible to use. The frets have been filed down, and new tuning pegs have been added. Because he has always experienced difficulty in tuning his Gibson, Iommi had several custom bridges constructed, and his current bridge raises the strings to a higher position than usual, bringing the open strings and 12-fret octaves into almost perfect sympathy. The bridge's height also prevents the lightweight strings he uses from constantly rattling against the fretboard.

"It's sort of an experimental guitar," Iommi says. "Everything that can be done to a guitar has been done to this one. That's probably why I like it, because I've got it exactly as I want it—apart from still having trouble with tuning."

The change from Fender to Gibson came one night when the band was playing in Germany, and one of the pickups went out on Tony's Stratocaster. Grudgingly, he snatched the Gibson—which he kept on stage for such emergencies—and since that time has never returned to a Fender of any model. The Gibson neck and fretboard appealed to him more than the Fender, as well as the ease with which he could bend notes. He now owns several Gibsons, including an old Les Paul with three pickups (with the original SG design), a newer model SG, and a Les Paul Junior (which Leslie West gave him as a present). Among his collection of acoustic instruments are a Gibson J-50 and an expensive Guild, though he confesses that the disarray over his entire house prevents him from really knowing what he owns.

All his guitars had to be switched around to accommodate his left-handedness. Tony now realizes that when he first started, he could have probably just turned a right-hand guitar around, and played it upside down. But he didn't, and now must either buy a left-handed guitar, or alter instruments to fit his needs. To add to his southpaw problem, Tony must also contend with the amputation he suffered years ago.

"You see, I can't use right-handed instruments now," he points out, "because I snipped the ends of my fingers off, and, on a Les Paul, you've got to get right up to the end of the guitar on a reversed right-handed instrument to hit the strings. Not many people know about the accident. It happened years ago when I was doing electric welding. One day, I had to cut this sheet metal before I welded. Somebody else used to do it, but I had to do it this day, because he didn't come into work. And it was a faulty switch or something—*thhhhhht!* I pulled my fingers out, and it just gripped the ends and pulled them off."

As fate would have it, the day of the accident was Tony's last day on the job before he was to have left for Germany with a rock outfit. Feeling completely lost, he decided to give up the guitar until a friend brought him a record of Django Reinhardt. After hearing what the brilliant gypsy guitarist did with just two fingers, Tony again took up the instrument.

"I had to start all over again," he recalls. "It was kind of a drag. I have to wear things now because the ends are so tender. It has helped me a little bit with my technique, though, because now I use my little finger a lot."

The "things" Tony wears are like little plastic thimbles that fit over the ends of the two digits. He's tried various sorts of adapters, but hasn't really come up with any that are totally comfortable. Frustration at times over the accident, an ill-sounding guitar, and a poor performance used to bring out violent reactions.

"Back then, I'd get annoyed, pick the guitar up, and smash it," he says. "I don't do that anymore, but, at first, I didn't think people realized how hard it was to learn to play like that. It involved a lot of determination, and a lot of hard work and practice. The accident happened over eight years ago—way before Sabbath or Tull—but when I joined Jethro they said, 'What are those things on your fingers?' When I told them, they were quite surprised to find I could play guitar with them. I've had to adopt a totally different way of playing. It's much easier when the flesh is there as it should be. Instead of, say, pulling a note, I have to sort of push it up to get a vibrato. The tips are a bit clumsy, and they slow me down and get in the way. I even have to wear leather on them to grip the strings. But it's just something I'll have to try and overcome."

Tony has also had to search for the right strings—ones that would-n't clink or buzz when pushed with his tips. By combining Ernie Ball light-gauge strings for the first and second strings, and Picato light-gauge strings for the remaining four, he has developed a set that's comfortable for both chording and solo playing. His strings are changed twice a week, but never right before a performance. Iommi feels that leaving them on any longer causes the strings to wear out over the frets, and makes them virtually impossible to tune. A very percussive player, Tony uses custom-made picks fashioned after normal Fender picks in shape, but which lie between thin and medium gauges.

Iommi explains that Black Sabbath tunes to a *D* on stage to get more depth.

"That's one of the reasons why I don't like using heavy-gauge strings," he adds, "because when I bend the strings they'll rip my bloody fingers apart. On acoustics, I like light-gauge strings, as well, because I can get a nice sound from them."

On stage, Tony uses no pedals at the present time, because he feels they do more harm than good. Because the band tours the United States so frequently, they must contend with the different systems of grounding. In England, their Laney amplifiers give maximum performance, but over here, the different ground

"DY-NO-MITE" DISCS!

Paranoid, Black Sabbath, 1970

Master of Reality, Black Sabbath, 1971

Volume 4, Black Sabbath, 1972

setup causes the stacks to hiss and growl and perform below average. Therefore, adding any sort of extra unit to the line causes extraneous buzzes. In England, Tony uses a wah-wah and a Minimoog, but found that using them in America caused a significant drop in amplifier power and sound. The group is now searching for an American-made system that won't plague them with those problems.

In the meantime, to accommodate for the ill performance of his Laney stacks in the US, Tony must set his amplifiers on full volume. The presence, middle, and treble knobs are also set to ten, with no bass on the amp whatsoever. The guitar volume is usually set on full—the better to unleash the thundering chords he hammers out—and the three-way pickup selector is set to the neck pickup for chords, and to the bridge pickup for soloing. In the studio, Iommi uses these same amp settings, but only one 100-watt Laney stack, rather than the four amp heads he uses onstage. For a particular solo, though, he'll use a Fender amplifier. On record, Tony delves into effects a little more than he does on stage, using a wah-wah, a Rotosound pedal, and various boosters and phasers.

Leo Kottke blew minds with his fingerstyle flurries on the 12-string guitar. (COURTESY OF *GUITAR PLAYER* MAGAZINE)

BY MICHAEL BROOKS

MARCH 1972

Leo Kottke

THERE'S A YOUNG FINGERSTYLE GUITARIST ON
the horizon who is fast becoming known to guitarists
through word of mouth and via his latest Capitol release,
Mudlark. Leo Kottke is a Georgia-born guitarist/vocalist
whose musical synthesis has integrated varying degrees
of ragtime, folk, bluegrass, country, and western and classical, and who has recently won membership in that
small clique of commercially tangent, self-taught guitarists that include John Fahey and Ry Cooder. His musical ideas were shaped from Pete Seeger, Jimmy Giuffre,
Grant Green, Mitch Greenhill, Fred Gerlach, and Burl
Ives, and his listening background also encompasses a
wide realm influences from Bach to Beethoven to Buddy
Holly. What makes Kottke significant among the thousands of guitarists today, are his 6- and 12-string fingerpicking styles formed from melody lines.

When did you start playing guitar?

About 12 years ago when I was sick. My folks bought
me one of those dime-store guitars to
fuss with—the kind of thing you
would order from the Sears catalog.

**What kind of music were you lis-
tening to then?**

Burl Ives. This was quite a while
ago, when I was about 13. I started
playing banjo about the same time I

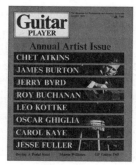

started the guitar, and that helped my guitar playing quite a bit.

Did you have lessons or anything?

I had eight years of trombone lessons, but I don't think they could apply.

That probably helped as far as music theory, though.

Yeah. I learned a little bit about organization. My organization tends to get really stale—at least to me. Lately, I've been playing more and more Bach stuff, because everything he writes is perfect. Just perfect. I always feel like a moron when I go back to try to write something myself after working on his music, but I do get a few ideas from playing it.

In most of your numbers, do you use three fingers for fingerpicking?

Usually, I'll use the thumb and three fingers if I'm playing some sort of form figure like an arpeggio. When I use the thumb in picking, it's just in unison with the second finger.

Do you normally use your thumb just for an alternating bass?

Yes, and I try to get it into the melody, as well.

When you fingerpick, do you normally assign the treble strings to each one of the three fingers you use to pick with, and then use the thumb to take care of the three bass strings?

I usually depend on my fingers for the first four strings, and the thumb for the bottom four—although many times, the fingers will also go for the fifth and sixth strings. It just depends on what kind chop I want. The fingers overlap a lot, and it's when they overlap that I have the most fun, because then I can break out of the "dead" thumb thing without losing the meter of the song.

You don't limit the thumb to just three bass strings then?

I try not to. The thumb is alternating on its octave of the pairs that I'm picking. In other words, instead of playing that lower octave, the thing that is picking up the melody is the octave string. It's not really a bass run, then—it sounds more like it's in the treble. It's kind of like the runs you hear a lot of banjo players doing.

Do you use fingerpicks?

Sometimes. When I amplify one of my 12-strings through an amp, I play with my fingernails and thumbpick. For my acoustic 12-string, I play with picks, and some of the things on my 6-string are played with picks. I don't like them though, because they're clumsy.

What kind of fingerpicks do you use when you're using them?

National, and a clear plastic Dobro thumbpick. I always light a match to the point of the thumbpicks to shorten them a little bit, because they're too long and too sharp when they're new.

Have you been through the old blues trip—the Charley Patton and Mississippi John Hurt-style runs?

No. I'm just now starting that trip. Some people I really appreciate are Joseph Spence, Blind Blake, and the Reverend Robert Wilkins. I'm trying to work out an arrangement of a thing Wilkins does called "Thank You, Jesus." I never listened to it before, because, first of all, I didn't know it was there. When I found that piece, it took me a long time to get used to the form.

When you say "the form," what do you mean?

Well, the blues form—all of that 12-bar repetition that goes on. You see, the things that I like to listen to are either classical, or they have a little bit of jazz in there.

> 66 You see, the things that I like to listen to are either classical, or they have a little bit of jazz in there. 99

What got you into the bottleneck guitar?

Let's see, the first time I heard slide was on a song about a flood on a record by Rolf Kahn and Eric Von Schmidt. I didn't like it at the time. Then, I remembered it a couple of years ago, and I started fooling around with a broken-off bottleneck, and I fell in love with the sound. Then, I started looking for other people who were playing it. John Fahey's "Poor Boy" was another tune that got me interested in playing bottleneck.

What guitars do you have?

I have a Gibson B45-12 12-string, a 1935 Martin 000-18 made in 1935, and an electric 12-string cutaway with a 28-inch scale that John Lundberg made for me in Berkeley. I've got about six other instruments, but most of them are in stages of disrepair or repair.

What kind of action do you have on your instruments?

My guitars are really hard to play, because I use very heavy strings, and I keep the action high. My big problem is just staying in tune when I play up the neck, because the strings are so heavy that they tend to sharp when I fret them. But I just feel more comfortable if I have to really yank to play. It feels more concrete if you have to work for it a little bit. Dick Rosmini once said that he didn't really start to play until the guitars he had that were easy to play were stolen, because then he couldn't depend on the guitar to carry him over.

Have you ever used an electric solidbody?

I do have one. I used it once in Chicago, and when I pulled it out, the whole audience groaned.

I'd like to get a good perspective on how you picked up your technique. Were there any factors you tried to emphasize more than others?

Yeah. I emphasized melody. I wanted to get to the point where *all* I was playing was melody. That's why I was so crazy about Pete Seeger, because everything he did was melodic. Everything I heard him do, I just had to learn—especially "Living in the Country." Now I'm getting kind of tired of that, and I want to learn some more rhythm.

In the recording studio, what are some of the idiosyncrasies that challenge you?

Oh, I lose my meter in the studio. I don't have anything to plug into, because they are such sterile places.

Have you done much session work?

No. I did it once or twice with really disappointing results. I think that doing sessions must be a grim way to make a living, because you must have to play an awful lot of trite music.

How much are you playing for yourself, and how much are you playing for the audience?

It's about one and the same. Unless I am in a grouchy mood, they never really separate. If I'm in a bad mood, and I'm really tired, then I just play for the audience, and it can get pretty boring when I'm not really enjoying myself. If I'm really pooped, I have to force myself through the first couple of songs. Then, I can get into it.

What is your musical goal?

I want to learn counterpoint. I would like to do more

"DY-NO-MITE" DISCS!

6- and 12-String Guitar, 1971

Mudlark, 1971

Leo Kottke, John Fahey & Peter Lang, 1974

interpretation as I am playing, instead of just reeling it off. Ultimately, I would like to learn how to play piano. I think if I could play piano at least as well as I play the guitar, it would probably be more satisfying. The piano is pretty dry-sounding to me, but everything is there. It doesn't have any limits to it. I would like to be able to exploit that.

Steve Lukather

THE FOLLOWING INTERVIEW IS BY JAS OBRECHT.

How did you come to start playing guitar?
My father bought me this old funky Kay acoustic guitar for my sev-

Steve Lukather was a preeminent session guitarist before forming the chart-topping band Toto in 1977.
(MARTY TEMME/ WIREIMAGE/GETTY IMAGES)

enth birthday. I started playing different instruments like drums and piano, but the guitar was always my best instrument over the years. At first I just copied records, and, as time went on, people would turn me on to hipper music. Like when I heard Jimi Hendrix the first time, I was just blown away. This was about the same time that Eric Clapton was playing with Cream, and I flipped out on that, too.

Were you playing electrics by then?

Yeah. I had an Astra-Tone guitar that my mom bought for me—it had three pickups. I got a Leo Krebs fuzz tone, and I was wailing through my Alamo amp. That was a really wild trip. Then, my parents bought me a fake Les Paul. They kept thinking, "Aw, he'll grow out of it—it's cute now." But I had been playing in a band with a bunch of older kids since I was 11, and playing guitar was something I really wanted to do, and I never gave up on it.

What kind of lessons did you take?

They were from Jimmy Wyble, who is a monster of a player. He got it together for me. I didn't know how to read a note when I started. He got me into positions on the guitar—notes, scales, and relationships. I could play pretty good rock and roll, but I didn't know anything about bebop or gut-

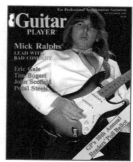

string stuff, and that's what Jimmy is a killer at.

What did he emphasize in your lessons?

Practice. He had me practicing everything, because I had so much to get together, it was scary. He said, "Keep your mind open to anything. Don't be stuck into a rock and roll thing, or jazz, or any other form of music. Just listen to it all." And that was something that stuck in my mind, and now I'm pro-everything.

> 66 Listen to what is going down on records. And it's not all written out—people get scared off by that so much. 99

How did you get into the studio scene?

I did my first record when I was 12. I was in junior high, and we had a little three-piece band. We were playing Hendrix-type stuff. The drummer's father was an engineer, and he took us into the studios and recorded us. Then, when I got older, I started getting a lot of calls to do demo tapes.

That's how I got my experience. About the time I was 17, I was like the kid guitar player who was pretty good for being a kid, but I wanted to really get it together. Then, I got to be friends with Larry Carlton, and he really helped me a lot in town.

My first record date came when I was 19. It was an overdub, and I was freaked out that my name would be on the same record as Dean Parks and other cats like that. Jay Graydon was the first heavy cat I ever sat next to. He sort of took me under his wing, and said, "Hey, kid, I'll show you what to do." Jay was really good to me, and I'll never forget it. He showed me tons of tricks. Jay also turned me on to some good amps, and he was the first guy I ever saw with a Roland Boss Chorus Ensemble. He also taught me the attitude to have on sessions—the "keep your eyes open" type of thing. It was sort of on-the-job training. He really got me a lot of dates, too. He'd say to people, "Call Lukather—he's the new kid in town. Let's give him a break."

Is that how you started getting most of your session dates?

Well, as far as session guys go, there weren't that many around at the time who could get a decent rock and roll sound, except for Jay Graydon. At this point, all the legendary cats—the Carltons, the Dean Parks[es], the Lee Ritenours—were doing their own albums, and devoting their time to production and writing. So when I hit the scene, there was a load of work. I was the only guy who would come in and turn his amp all the way up. Some of the other guys around just wouldn't do that. They'd turn their amps up just a little bit—like on the verge of breakup—and say, "Yeah, this is the rock and roll sound you want, right?" And it would sound lame. That's part of the reason I started working a lot.

What do you take with you to a session?

I have a whole load of equipment. My session setup is different than my live setup. I have two blackface Fender amps—a Deluxe and a Princeton. Paul Rivera beefed them up, putting midrange controls and some other stuff on them. He also made me a pedalboard that's really sophisticated.

Going from left to right, what effects are in it?

Far left, I have a Goodrich volume pedal that I work with either foot. Next to that is an MXR Dyna Comp that has a buffer amp inside so I don't lose any highs or volume. Next to that is a Roland Boss Chorus Ensemble that Paul changed so I would get less distortion and a cleaner sound. Then, I have an Ibanez AD-230 Multi Flanger, an Eventide Harmonizer, a Roland RE-201 Space Echo, an MXR Ten-Band Graphic Equalizer, a Cry Baby wah-wah pedal, and an MXR Flanger. I've also got a Dan Armstrong Orange Squeezer, which is a compressor that fits on my Strat. It sounds unbelievable—very pop. I can get that Jeff Baxter type of sound.

What guitars do you take?

My favorite guitar out of my whole collection is a 1958 Gibson goldtop Les Paul. It's a dynamite guitar. I also have a Strat-style guitar that Mike McGuire of Valley Arts Guitar made it for me. It's a really beautiful guitar with a Boogie Bodies bird's-eye maple neck and a mahogany body by Schecter, and three Schecter pickups. It has a rosewood fingerboard, because my hand has a tendency to slip off maple fingerboards—although I do think maple looks better. That guitar also has a whang bar, so I can get the Jimi Hendrix, Eddie Van Halen, and Jeff Beck trip with it. I also take a 1970 sunburst Gibson ES-335, which is stock except for wider frets, Schaller machine heads, and a Schaller bridge. These are good bridges—they don't slip. I have a tendency to wear out bridge inserts at the high E, B, and G strings, so I have to change them about once a month.

What s your onstage setup with Toto?

I use my pedalboard a lot, and I just have a stereo line going out of the Roland Boss Chorus Ensemble to the amps. I have three amps—a 100-watt Marshall that has an extra preamp control on it, a 50-watt Marshall, and an Ampeg VT-22. My main onstage guitar is the Les Paul goldtop.

What kind of picks and strings do you use?

I like the tiny Fender jazz picks—they're very hard. I hold them between my thumb and first finger, and with the point out. I string my electrics with Ernie Ball Super Slinkys, and my Martin acoustic with Martin Lights.

What advice would you give someone wanting to become a studio player?

All I can say is, think about all the aspects of it, and listen to those cats. Listen to what is going down on records. And it's not all written out—people get scared off by that so much. They think, "God, I have to be an incredible reader to do this." When I started doing dates, my reading was the pits. It got better over time, but I was lucky enough to get gigs on my level of reading. As time went on, I started getting harder gigs, and, by then, I could make it. Almost all the dates have chord charts, but I'd say only about 30 to 40 percent require reading.

Most of the time, you've got to make up your own stuff—which is cool, because it is a challenge musically. It's not like you're a robot, and just have to turn on the old brain and play what's on the paper.

There's a big difference in what kind of sessions you're doing, too. I want to clarify that. There are movie dates, TV dates, or records. The difference is the pressure. With movie dates, there's intense reading pressure, and if you're one minute late for a movie date, you're hanging up about 100 people. Tommy Tedesco is in control of that stuff. Like, he can screw around on a date and be crazy, and nobody says anything to him. If a new guy

"DY-NO-MITE" DISCS!

Toto, Toto, 1978

Hydra, Toto, 1979

was to come along and be crazy on a date, you'd probably never see him again. There's a lot of protocol involved, too. You've got to realize where you're at, and who you're sitting next to.

Are most record dates the same?

Well, there are two kinds of record dates. One kind is that you show up, and maybe three hours later, they are still getting the kick drum sound. Talk about relaxed dates—they don't even have charts. Then, there's the other kind where it's pretty together, and you've got the music. As far as solos, they're usually not written out. They come from the guitarist. They cut a track, you overdub a solo—or maybe a few solos—and they pick one.

Do you ever have trouble thinking up something to play?

Not really. If I'm really hung up, I'll think of something I've played before. I hate to be repetitive, but I think everyone is repetitive in their own way. That's what makes a style, really.

How has being in Toto changed your life?

Oh, man—it's changing my life 100 percent. It has made me secure. I'm in a band with some of the best cats I could think of—Jeff Porcaro, David Paich, Steve Porcaro, and David Hungate. I've also been writing all different kinds of tunes, so I'm really enjoying it all.

After a near-fatal brain aneurysm in 1980, Pat Martino had to learn to play guitar again. (VERYL OAKLAND/RETNA LTD.)

BY ROBERT YELIN

SEPTEMBER 1973

Pat Martino

THE CITY THAT SPAWNED SUCH GREAT JAZZ
guitarists as Eddie Lang, Dennis Sandole, and
Thornel Schwartz, also gave us, 29 years ago, Pat
Martino.

As a youngster in Philadelphia, Pat was introduced
to music by his father, a singer. There were many
father/son trips to the Red Hill Inn, where they heard
such jazz greats as Art Blakey, Art Farmer, John Coltrane,
and, especially, guitarist Johnny Smith.

At 11, the youngster who was eventually to play
with Jimmy Smith, Jack McDuff, Groove Holmes, and
Jimmy McGriff, got his first guitar. He had little formal
training, but through desire, he taught himself the rudiments of playing and music. Pat listened avidly to every
Johnny Smith album in the house, copying all he could.
Shortly after, Pat began lessons with Dennis Sandole,
whom he still considers his greatest influence.

Pat turned professional at 15, going on tour with the
rhythm-and-blues bands of Lloyd
Price, Willis Jackson, and others. It
was while with Jackson that the guitarist recorded his first jazz solos,
still using the family name of Azzara.
(His father worked under the name
Martino, and Pat took it for his own
after leaving the Jackson band.)

Though Pat never attended high school, he doesn't regret it for a second, feeling that this period on the road was his schooling.

At 22, after recording often as a sideman, Martino released his first album, *El Hombre*, for Prestige. This record clearly showed that Pat was not only at home with the blues idiom which had been so much a part of his life, but that he also could fit in well with the pure jazz form. His octave playing on the album was considered by many to be the finest and warmest-sounding since Wes Montgomery. Pat later recorded four more albums for Prestige, some containing East Indian–influenced music, others utilizing an electric 12-string.

How did you first become interested in the guitar?

There was always a guitar lying around the house. My dad played basic chords and just fooled around with it. He enjoyed listening to Johnny Smith, Django, and Eddie Lang records, and made sure I heard them, too. Eddie Lang gave my father some lessons. So, by my being exposed to the guitar, it was just a matter of time before I got drawn into playing it. Once I started actually playing guitar, it completely fascinated me.

Did any players influence you?

Of course—Johnny Smith, Wes Montgomery, and just about any guitar player I ever listened to.

What did Smith's playing offer you?

Precision! Precision and cleanliness and getting over what you want to say without laboring over impediments. I am always concerned with the present moment, and when I was listening and viewing Smith's mastery of the guitar, I seriously wanted to become another Johnny Smith. I copied all I could comprehend from his albums. But, when I started studying with Dennis Sandole, Dennis made me realize that if Smith stopped making records, I'd have to stop playing. The most important thing about a player is that what he plays is recognizable—cleanly executed with articulation and dynamics. Smith's playing has all these aspects. Another great thing about his playing is that he has kept his identity. You can always recognize his playing and his sound.

Don't you find that studying a man's playing is mechanical, and only covers half the picture? The other half concerns the forces that make them express as they do.

True—especially with the younger cats. They don't take into consideration that when they are listening to a musician, they are actually listening to a stronger force—a force that the musician is in a relationship to. For instance, that musician may be a theologian, philosopher, mathematician, or politician, but the listeners only see their Mel Bay and Nick Manoloff books. This isn't their fault—it's just a matter of reality. Hopefully, with time and wisdom, they will learn that there are more realities than expressing yourself in music. For instance, how could you analyze John Coltrane's music without being aware of what he was in relationship to?

Are there forces in your playing that are not musical?

A lot. They are based on form, symmetry, and division. For example, there are only four positions on the guitar before you have duplication of notes. And there are only four registers, too. The diminished chord shows you that in a capsule: You have four diminished chords going up the fingerboard before you hit the fifth—which is a duplication. That's because the diminished chord is the division of one octave into four equal parts. The guitar is totally based on chromaticism. A lot of players see the guitar as an arrangement of frets. I, instead, see it as a reality where the fingerboard can be broken down into five chromatic scales and a duplication. Therefore, it reduces the terms of redundancy.

What other ways can you avoid this repetition?

I have systems of equations. They deal with things like rotation, which is a great way of overcoming repetition in music. Take a chromatic scale from C to C, which is a 12-point sequence, and write it on the staff. Directly below that, divide it into a six-point sequence, which will give you whole tones. Below that, pull out the notes that are in the sesqui-tone [minor thirds] of the diminished sequence, and below that the di-tone [major thirds] and, finally, the tri-tone [flatted fifths], which is the division of the 12-tone in half. Then, connect every point of reference from the C to the F♯. You will then arrive at a 12-point star which shows a balance that permeates music itself. It's analogous to one point of music leading to another to create an idea, or, in this case, a picture. We're not taught to see things of this nature, but this is exactly what I'm interested in. This balance is a binding factor that causes something to be in accordance with equilibrium. It's these things that I base all my studies and analyses upon. So you see, it really isn't the guitar that I'm involved with. The guitar is only an instrument, and you soon exhaust its limits. The guitar has only four octaves, and when you're dealing with the divisions of music itself, you need at least 11.

With all this in mind, do you still consider yourself a guitarist?

In the first five or six years of my playing I did, but not after that. I'm an observer of environment—including the guitar. I see the guitar in everything. I think that, at certain levels of performance, the player becomes de-personalized by the instrument, and I don't particularly care for that. It's hard to retain one's identity when you're locked into the identity of a machine.

Are you a jazz musician?

No. Jazz is a way of life—not an idiom of music. Jazz is spontaneous improvisation. If you ever walk out of your house with nowhere to go—just walking for the pleasure of it and observing what's around you—you'll find that you improvise. Everyone in life improvises. Jazz is just relative degrees of improvisation.

What does music and the guitar mean to you?

Music is my discipline for my life. I look at the guitar not as an instrument to be mastered, but as a discipline to see life through.

What is the most difficult phase of playing the guitar?

Learning to get away from thinking of the problems of fingering and picking technique. You really don't have to relate to all that, because, after a while, it becomes natural.

If Wes Montgomery hadn't brought octaves to the forefront, do you think you would have become aware of them on your own?

Yes—because I became very aware of the textural aspects of putting things together in terms of note clusters and octave forms. It's an eventuality, as soon as you look into more classical thoughts. When you consider yourself as a density with a parameter for control, as a musician, you're in direct proximity to where octaves come from. If you're not dealing with chords, per se, you're dealing with more ambiguous forms of cluster. Then, you can take into consideration the five-tone unit, the four-tone unit, and the three-tone units, the pentachord, hexachord, tetrachord, trichord, and the dyad. As soon as you get into the dyad, you'll immediately find octaves.

What do you find are your students' most common problems in playing guitar?

Many times, a student has to learn patience and understanding. He may be oblivious or non-sensitive to the reality of where he is, and what he's involved in. Teaching, leading, and guiding are when you can get a student to confront his own inadequacies. Sometimes, a very short lesson will do as much as a very long one. In teaching, you also have the searchers and the finders. The searchers get caught up in the syndrome of searching, but they can't recognize when they've found something. These are professional students—not players. On the other hand, you have the finders who are not interested in searching or questioning and answering. They are just interested in being involved. These people are really alive. They are the players.

In the music you write, you don't use key signatures. Why not?

I don't relate to them. I see everything harmonically. I see things in a more 12-tone sense. Chromaticism plays a heavy part in my music. You have to free yourself from locked-in and false perspectives, and use your imagination to create your own breathing on your instrument. This is where your creativity abides. When you create an idea, however, you must also create an audience for it. I believe, though, that nothing is totally new. Only what is forgotten seems new.

Do you know which direction your writing and playing will take you in the foreseeable future?

I know exactly where it's going to take me. I can't say what it's going to do for me materialistically, but my writing and playing are going to lead me right where I'm at now. With a certain amount of study, you can reach a level where you can remain stationary, and get a view of things around you. I call this level "peace," and this is where I'd like to remain.

"DY-NO-MITE" DISCS!

Footprints, 1972

Consciousness, 1974

Exit, 1976

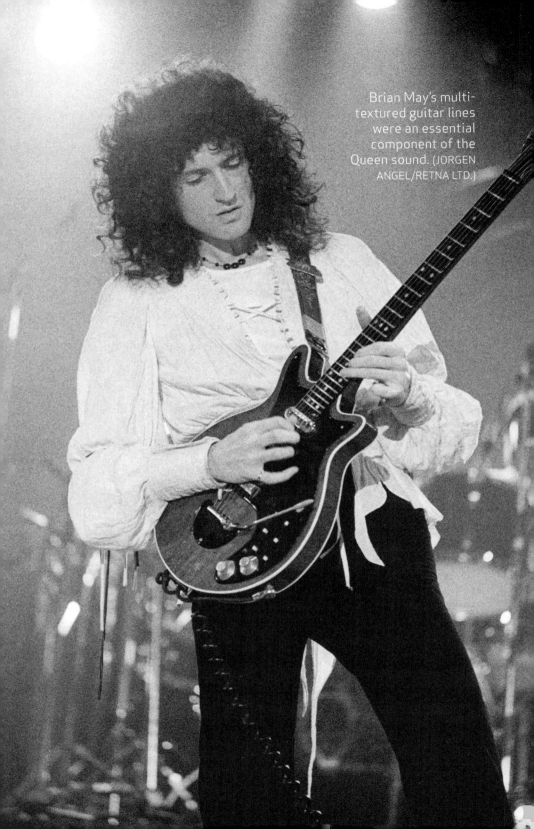

Brian May's multi-textured guitar lines were an essential component of the Queen sound. (JORGEN ANGEL/RETNA LTD.)

Brian May

BRIAN MAY IS THE 27-YEAR-OLD GUITARIST *for Queen, the English "metal" quartet. When only 17, he built his own electric guitar and has been using it ever since. He has recorded three albums with Queen on the Elektra label. The following questions were submitted by Ron Franklin of Los Angeles, California.*

When and why did you first start playing?

I must have been about seven or eight years old, and I remember seeing a film about Tommy Steele. My father played the ukulele, and he taught me a few chords on that instrument. When I got a guitar, I just converted those four-string chords to a six-string guitar.

You made your own guitar?

I made my first "electric" guitar by winding wire around a magnet, and putting the magnet on my first acoustic guitar. Then, my friends started buying electric guitars, and I realized I needed something better, so I did a lot of experimenting, trying different tremolo designs, and set out to make the thing.

What type of amp system do you use?

I use Vox AC30s, which are old English amps they've just started building again. It's a 30-watt amp with two 12" speakers built into one cabinet. I use six of them on stage. I

have an Echoplex—which has its time control specially extended so I can get long delays. The delay signal comes back into a second amp, and I have another Echoplex that goes back into yet another amp. I have two amps for each echo unit. The only other pedal I use is a booster, which is on all the time. It's a one-stage preamp that's used to get a bit more signal. I made that device, as well.

> 66 I made my first 'electric' guitar by winding wire around a magnet, and putting the magnet on my first acoustic guitar. 99

What are some of the features of your guitar?

It has a very far-reaching tremolo—the bottom string can go down an octave. The dials and switches are all ordinary things you can buy in an electric shop. The pickups are Burns, but I took them apart and rewound them, and now they're a bit higher impedance than they were. They don't whistle as much. Everything else was built from scratch—the frets, fingerboard, and tremolo. The guitar has a mahogany neck that came from an old fireplace, and the body is oak—very heavy old oak. It's a semi-acoustic. Although it hasn't got any holes, there are a lot of hollow places in it. It's quite a live guitar—it feeds back very easily.

What kind of strings and pick do you use?

Rotosound, usually. Sometimes, Picato. The gauges are .008, .010, .011, .022, .030, and .034 or .036. They're pretty light. For picks, I generally use English sixpences, which are something like an American

"DY-NO-MITE" DISCS!

Queen II, Queen, 1974

Sheer Heart Attack, Queen, 1974

A Night at the Opera, Queen, 1975

nickel. I used to use regular picks, but I like them very stiff, so that all the flexibility comes from the fingers.

Who would you cite as your biggest influence?

Jimi Hendrix was my idol—for his style and his feel. I think he made the guitar something better than it was before he came along. He was the ultimate guitarist. I don't think anyone has ever come near him.

Mahavishnu John McLaughlin with his "Double Rainbow" guitar, handmade by Rex Bogue.
(COURTESY OF *GUITAR PLAYER* MAGAZINE)

BY VIC TRIGGER

NOVEMBER 1972

John McLaughlin

I WAS TO MEET MAHAVISHNU—WHOM I FIRST
addressed as John—at three pm, but since he hadn't
as yet arrived, I began looking over his equipment, which
had just been set up. He would be playing through 100-
watt Marshall Super Lead amp and three Marshall bottoms. On the floor was a DeArmond 602 volume pedal,
the only pedal he would use.

Violinist Jerry Goodman was the only musician to
arrive on time. McLaughlin was next, though, and proceeded to sit down and play drums. He said he was
happy to do the interview, but wasn't interested in dis-
cussing technical matters. But as the time grew later,
Mahavishnu grew more and more concerned over the
whereabouts of the rest of his band, so we agreed to
meet after the evening's show.

At nine pm, the musicians were in place and
McLaughlin walked on stage with his double-necked
Gibson. The group mostly played tunes from the *Inner
Mounting Flame* album, sounding
amazingly like the record. Mahavishnu
played most of his leads on the 6-
string neck, and most of the arpeggiat-
ed chords on the 12-string neck.

Following the five minutes of
standing ovations and a final encore,
I met McLaughlin in the dressing

room where he was relaxing, eating fruit.

How long did it take to put this band together?

It took me about two months to find all the musicians. I knew the drummer and the violinist, and I'd heard of the others through friends. Miroslav Vitous [bassist] told me about Jan Hammer [keyboards].

Wasn't Vitous on *Spaces*, your first album after you broke with Miles Davis?

I haven't broken with Miles, in fact, we've done other sessions together. I was never *with* him in the sense most people think. And I wasn't with Larry Coryell on that *Spaces* album. It and *Devotion* were both studio recordings.

With all your playing experience, what do you find yourself falling back on the most?

Everything! I grew to where I am, and I use everything in balance. As I grow more, my playing will change as my being changes. I draw on all present things, and on what is beyond me.

When you solo, is it total self-concentration, or is it open concentration on the entire band?

Open. You open yourself to the things around you. Of course, it depends on the state of consciousness you're in—how deep and how high. I've been in states of consciousness where I'm not the creator. Then I just play.

What do you think of your solos on *Jack Johnson* and earlier albums?

Those were a long time ago. That was me then, but what I'm doing now is what best represents me. Of course, my development is well represented by those albums, because music is the only language I speak. I am learning the language of silence and meditation—the highest of languages.

Is communication what you want to do?

Yes! I want to move people. When I play, I want people to feel what is inside them. Those people tonight were clapping for what they feel inside themselves. And that's what I want to do, only deeper, purer, and purer.

Many people consider you a rock guitarist. Do you?

I don't care what people call me. I don't care what they call the music. We just get up there and play. It's like, people ask me what kind of music we play, and I say, "You listen, then you can call it anything you want." There are people who consider themselves Mahavishnu

Rock and Roll Freaks. That's great. I'd rather play for rock and roll audiences than jazz audiences anyway. Jazz listeners are too narrow—too purist for us. Rock audiences are more open.

How do you approach your improvisation?

When there is a desire to express something, there is a need, and out of that need it is born. Like, when you're carving and you say, "That's not right." You take away some, you add some. The total sound is the concern. But, sometimes, you don't carve out the right amount, because you can't always have great performances. Like meditating, you don't always have an incredible meditation every time. It would be like having a sumptuous feast every time you ate. You have to eat a little bread and water—be a little frugal. Frugal soup.

> 66 I draw on all present things, and on what is beyond me. 99

Is the desire to utilize this approach of yours born out of a need to?

It is born out of your dissatisfaction with your lot—dissatisfaction with what you're doing, and your lack of fulfillment. Most people don't fulfill their desires, let alone their aspirations. But they can if they want.

But what if you feel your desires are being hampered by the musicians you're playing with?

If you feel you're being dragged down by them, then your attitude is too passive, for a start, and with negative overtones. It's your duty to inspire your fellow musicians. It's especially your duty to inspire your fellow man, because the inspiration is within you and within me. And, to inspire you have to aspire.

Did your spiritual involvement begin after *Jack Johnson*?

I think I had just become a disciple in New York when that was recorded. You might say I was just born.

Would you explain "Mahavishnu?"

When you become a disciple, you have a Master. Mine is Sri Chinmoy. At some point he gives you a name, and that name has a very strong spiritual significance. It relates directly to the soul, and defines your existence and your whole body. Like you have certain qualities in your personality that are dominant, another person has other ones. These qualities must manifest themselves in your Being. The name embodies these qualities, and the more you are called the name, the more you use the name, and the more the name helps you. Mahavishnu is an Indian god—Maha the Creator, and Vishnu the Preserver.

Do you feel more satisfaction from your playing now than before?

I have been evolving and growing all the time. As I evolve more, my music evolves more, and I feel more fulfillment. It's a constant process. Does meditation help eliminate distractions while playing? It helps my entire life. But, to eliminate distractions you have to live for something else—God, ideally. By doing that you don't become self-oriented, but become *selflessly* oriented. Once you rid yourself of the false ego, you lose your self in the music. And the moment you lose your self in the music is the moment you are getting somewhere, and the moment you start getting somewhere is the moment you begin to find your self. Losing your self.

On a good night, when you lose your self, do you perform unconsciously?

Of course. Music is way beyond the mind. You're conscious of what you're doing, but you're being moved by something greater. When I'm completely lost is when the music is the most incredible.

To what can a person listen to hear musicians like yourself?

Indian musicians! I am more and more influenced by Indian culture. I surround myself with their music and ideas.

What can a guitarist study to better understand and appreciate your music?

I'm not a musician for musicians. I'm a musician for non-musicians. That's what I want to be, and that's what I'll always want to be. What is a musician for, if he isn't for the non-musician? I'm a musician. I'm the ears of humanity. I listen on behalf of humanity. Most people's roles in this divine drama on earth is to do something else, but they love

"DY-NO-MITE" DISCS!

My Goal's Beyond, 1970

Love Devotion Surrender, 1972

Inner Worlds, Mahavishnu Orchestra, 1975

music so I am here for them. Musicians are here for people who can't hear, and painters are here for people who can't see, so they can *learn* to hear and see.

June Millington and her sister Jean formed Fanny—one of the first all-female rock bands—in 1969. (COURTESY OF JUNE MILLINGTON)

BY MICHAEL PIERCE

MARCH 1973

June Millington

FOR A SEX THAT PEOPLES A LITTLE MORE than half the world, it's quite surprising how few women have become rock musicians. Notwithstanding society's acceptability of females playing violins, violas, and other classical instruments, women have always been in a minority when they pick up on the guitar. But the guitar is a people's instrument, and making that statement in today's rock scene is Fanny—an all-female rock band that is not out to prove anything other than music is fun.

Fanny starts with the riffs of June Millington's 1956 Gibson Les Paul played through a Fender Bassman. It's that kind of sound. For the smaller halls, she plays a Fender Deluxe, but can still achieve that Bassman sound because she has modified her Les Paul to include a master volume control and a booster. And as she has learned to guitar almost totally by ear, her technical and theory background, while limited, doesn't interfere with her perception on how a lead should be compatible with the band's overall sound. One of her major complaints in rock music is that solos are often boring, and are frequently out of context with what the group should really be trying to convey.

While living in the Philippines,

attending a strict Spanish parochial school, June's initial interest in the guitar was mere fascination.

"Some chick bought a guitar, and I heard strains of guitar music coming out of the next room," she says. "I freaked, and thought, 'God, that girl must be so lucky to be able to play the guitar.'"

Just before leaving the Philippines, her mother bought her one, and June began to learn the rudiments of guitar from a stateside boyfriend. At this point, June was without influences—totally motivated by the sound of the instrument. Being a shy, quiet-natured young lady, June found it difficult to get it together with other guitarists for fear of embarrassment. She was much more into school—a more serene head trip than the field of entertainment. It was at a time, when the Beatles and surf music filled the speakers of AM radios coast-to-coast, that June began to break from her fragile shell. Playing hootenannies and going steady with a boy in a band, eventually led June into playing between the sets of her boyfriend's group. What mattered most was the social aspect of playing, and just simply having good fun.

> **❝ I think melodic first, and if you are an exceptional guitar player, you can make it disjointed and melodic at the same time, but that's a difficult trip to play. ❞**

"It certainly wasn't what it is now, like, 'Let's really get into the music,' and all that," says June. "It wasn't so much about technique."

Then, came the proving grounds. Housecleaning for the wife of the owner of the Heavenly Valley ski resort in California's Lake Tahoe, June and her sister, Jean, got a gig playing acoustic folk at the resort's mountain-top restaurant. They played every night for one summer, and learned a lot about entertaining. Then, at 17, June was in her senior year of high school, when she got a call, "I play drums. Do you want to start a group?"

"Well, why not?" was June's and her sister's reply.

Because June is the older sister, and wanted to play guitar, Jean began playing bass. After the band started rehearsing, June gave up her pawnshop electric for a Gretsch, which she played for a couple of years before moving to a Gibson ES-355. The group was called Wild Honey, and the members went to Los Angeles to get more gigs. But Wild Honey couldn't stand the strain of moving, and soon it disbanded. In the last months of the band, June was asked to play lead guitar.

"I really balked," she explains, "because I didn't want to play lead. I was actually scared, you know. I thought what everybody else thought—that a chick couldn't play lead. I was really inhibited."

But she did make the attempt, beginning by listening to records, and also by taping things, then slowing down the tapes to figure out what the lead guitar was doing. She did that night and day for a year. Why the sudden dedication? Once June started listening, she began to develop not only an ear for the sound of lead guitar, but a yearning to know more and more about lead.

"I'd learn a little bit, and then I'd want to learn more," she says. "And then it became an obsession. It was really far-out."

She used the same approach when she wanted to play slide guitar, except that she tried to learn directly from other players, as well.

"Lowell George of Little Feet played slide, and he was good at it, and I kind of got the feeling from watching him," she says. "I used to go through the trip of asking people, 'Would you teach me?' But it never worked, so I just watched, and then went home and tried it for myself. Once I had tried it, then I could go back and ask the person more specific questions. You see, I used to have some sort of fantasy in my mind where somebody would just sit me down and show me everything he knew, and then I'd have it together. But it never worked that way."

When June plays lead, she doesn't come to the forefront with overwhelmingly extended lead-guitar solos.

"Most of the time," she says, "when I listen to guys do long solos, I don't think it sounds that good. I get bored myself, so I figure if *I* don't dig it, why should I put that on other people? I'm not into putting people on. There have just been so many times when we've listened to a group, and said, 'Yeah, he's pretty good, and he's really fast, but it just isn't saying anything.'"

June has definite ideas as to what a guitar solo should be, and what it should not be. As far as her own solos, June likes "Think About the Children," although she doesn't feel the sound was right.

"I think melodic first, and if you are an exceptional guitar player, you can make it disjointed and melodic at the same time, but that's a difficult trip to play," she says. "It also has to do with rhythm and syncopation with all the notes."

Regarding her own listening enjoyment, June stands in admiration of Jimi Hendrix's "Little Wing" solo, as well as much of the works of Muddy Waters, Howlin' Wolf, Robert Johnson, Albert Collins, Wes Montgomery, Little Milton, Les Paul, John McLaughlin, and Ry Cooder.

Because she finds it a bit difficult to compose on the electric guitar, she prefers acoustic. And even though she took a little theory in college, she keeps the entire song in her head until the composition is finished. Her writing realm is in thirds and fifths, but she also likes dissonance "when it's the right time." Her best songs, she feels, "are the ones that just happen, like 'You've Got a Home.'"

In arranging songs, the group works fairly close together, but as June mentions, "Sometimes, I'll be really strong and assert myself, because I've written the song, or I have certain ideas I want to get across. But Nickey [Barclay, piano/organ] and I are the most forward about trying things out—even though Jean [bass] and Alice [de Buhr, drums] have a definite say in everything. I suppose it's more democratic than anything else."

June sees Fanny's strong point as its versatility.

"There are a lot of musical elements in the group," she explains. "Nickey's and my musical tastes are so different that it's unreal. She was into Procol Harum really heavy, and I never was. I was into Motown, but a lot of Motown really disgusts her. She loves Rod Stewart and I don't. I love Neil Young. She hates him. It just goes on and on. But it's cool, because we write totally different from each other. It clashes a lot, but when we get it together, it's groovy. Another thing is that we have a good rhythm section, and we are all good musicians. We didn't have a

"DY-NO-MITE" DISCS!

Fanny, Fanny, 1970

Fanny Hill, Fanny, 1972

Mother's Pride, Fanny, 1973

particularly strong and distinctive lead-vocal sound, but I think we've developed one now. I've been taking vocal lessons in Los Angeles from a guy named Dean Rhodus. He's really good, and that should help make us stronger."

Unusual in lead playing, June uses a fingerpick on her middle finger in combination with a Herco flatpick. One little trick she gets off on is turning the pick around and using the perforated side against the string for a "raspy sound." The explanation for the additional pick is: "I can play two notes at a time if I want, and cut into some semi-finger-picking licks." While playing lead, June also uses her fourth finger. She plays in G tuning [low to high, D, G, D, G, B, D], and her only outboard effects are a no-name wah-wah from Holland and a Leslie rotary speaker—although her Les Paul is armed with a coil-tap switch (installed by Jeff Baxter of Valley Sound in Los Angeles) to get a "light and funky" Stratocaster-type sound. To finish off her equipment lineup, June uses Ernie Ball strings, gauged .010, .012, .016, .026, .036, .046.

"The best sound is a natural sound with a good guitar and a good amp," she says. "That may sound a little hypocritical because I'm running my guitar through a Leslie on some things, but in a four-piece band I have to change the sound a little."

Into musical directions, June just wants to be able to try to play a little bit of everything, and she never figures on settling on one particular style.

"It's because I'm so spaced out being an Aries and all that I'm the one in the group who likes to try everything," she explains. "But it's kind of groovy, too, because the group selects what we'll do out of all the things I want to do. Sometimes, I even get into doing music I would have never before considered. I never used to do country music before, and now I dig a lot of it. And I never used to dig the blues, but now I dig it, and I dig R&B and jazz and pop and all that stuff. I think every facet of music can be good. This is what the group has taught me."

Jimmy Page with the 1959 sunburst Les Paul he dubbed as "Number 1." (JORGEN ANGEL/RETNA LTD.)

BY STEVE ROSEN

JULY 1977

Jimmy Page

CONDUCTING AN INTERVIEW WITH JIMMY Page, lead guitarist and producer/arranger for England's notorious hard-rock band Led Zeppelin, amounts very nearly to constructing a mini-history of British rock and roll. Perhaps one of Zeppelin's more outstanding characteristics is its endurance, intact (no personnel changes since its inception) through an extremely tumultuous decade involving not only rock, but popular music in general. Since 1969, the group's four members—Page, bass player John Paul Jones, vocalist Robert Plant, and drummer John Bonham—have produced eight albums (two are doubles) of original and often revolutionary compositions with a heavy-metal sound. For as long as the band has been an entity, their records—coupled with several well-planned and highly publicized European and American tours—have exerted a profound and acutely recognizable influence on rock groups and guitar players on both sides of the Atlantic. Page's carefully calculated guitar frenzy, engineered through the use of distortion, surrounds Plant's expressive vocals to create a tension and excitement rarely matched by Zeppelin's numerous emulators.

But the prodigious contributions of James Patrick Page, born in 1945 in

Middlesex, England, date back to well before the formation of his present band. His work as a session guitarist earned him so lengthy a credit list (some sources cite Jimmy as having been on 50 to 90 percent of the records released in England during 1963–65) that he himself is no longer sure of each and every cut on which he played. Even without the exact number of his vinyl encounters known, the range of his interaction as musician and sometime producer with the landmark groups and individuals of soft and hard rock is impressive and diverse: the Who, Them, various members of the Rolling Stones, Donovan, and Jackie DeShannon, to name a few. In the mid-'60s, Page joined one of the best-known British rock bands, the Yardbirds, leading to a legendary collaboration with rock/jazz guitarist Jeff Beck. When the Yardbirds disbanded in 1968, Page was ready to start his own group. According to Jimmy, at the initial meeting of Led Zeppelin, the sound of success was already bellowing through the amps, and the musicians' four-week introductory period resulted in *Led Zeppelin*, their first of many gold-record-winning LPs.

Let's try to begin at the beginning. When you first started playing, what was going on musically?

I got really stimulated by hearing early rock and roll, and knowing that something was going on that was being suppressed by the media—which it really was at the time. You had to stick by the radio, and listen to overseas radio to even hear good rock records—Little Richard and things like that. The record that made me want to play guitar was "Baby, Let's Play House" by Elvis Presley. I just sort of heard two guitars and bass and thought, "Yeah, I want to be part of this." There was just so much vitality and energy coming out of it.

When did you get your first guitar?

When I was about 14. It was all a matter of trying to pick up tips and stuff. There weren't many method books, really—apart from jazz, which had no bearing on rock and roll whatsoever at that time. But that first guitar was a Grazioso, which was like a copy of a Stratocaster. Then, I got a real Stratocaster, and then one of those Gibson "Black Beauties"—which stayed with me for a long time until some thieving magpie took it to his nest. That's the guitar I did all the '60s sessions on.

What music did you play when you first started?

I wasn't really playing anything properly. I just knew a few bits of solos and things—not much. I just kept getting records and learning that way. It was the obvious influences at the beginning: Scotty Moore,

James Burton, Cliff Gallup—he was Gene Vincent's guitarist—and Johnny Weeks. Those seemed to be the most sustaining influences until I began to hear blues guitarists Elmore James, B. B. King, and people like that. Basically, that was the start—a mixture of rock and blues. Then, I stretched out a lot more, and I started doing studio work. I had to branch out, and I did. I might do three sessions a day— a film session in the morning, and then there'd be something like a rock band, and then maybe a folk session in the evening. I didn't know *what* was coming! But it was a really good disciplinary area to work in—the studio. And it also gave me a chance to develop on all of the different styles.

Were you playing acoustic guitar during your session period?

Yes. I had to do it on studio work. And you come to grips with it very quickly, too—very quickly, because it's what is expected. There was a lot of busking in the earlier days, but, as I say, I had to come to grips with it, and it was a good schooling.

You were also using the Les Paul for those sessions?

The Gibson Les Paul Custom—the "Black Beauty." I was one of the first people in England to have one, but I didn't know that then. I just saw it on the wall, had a go with it, and it was good. I traded a Gretsch Chet Atkins I'd had before for the Les Paul.

What kinds of amplifiers were you using for session work?

A small Supro, which I used until someone—I don't know who— smashed it up for me. I'm going to try to get another one. It's like a Harmony amp, I think, and all of *Led Zeppelin* was done on that.

Can you describe some of your musical interaction with Jeff Beck during the Yardbirds period?

Sometimes it worked really great, and sometimes it didn't. There were a lot of harmonies that I don't think anyone else had really done—not like we did. The Stones were the only ones who got into two guitars going at the same time from old Muddy Waters records. But we were more into solos, rather than a rhythm thing. The point is, you've got to have the parts worked out, and I'd find that I was doing what I was supposed to, while something totally different would be coming from Jeff. That was all right for the areas of improvisation, but there were other parts where it just did not work. You've got to under- stand that Beck and I came from the same sort of roots. If you've got things you enjoy, then you want to do them—to the horrifying point where we'd done *Led Zeppelin* with "You Shook Me," and then I heard *he'd* done "You Shook Me" on *Truth.* I was terrified, because I thought they'd be the same. But I hadn't even known he'd done it, and he hadn't known that we had.

What kind of guitar were you using on the first Led Zeppelin album?

A Telecaster. I used the Les Paul with the Yardbirds on about two numbers, and a Fender for the rest. You see, the Les Paul Custom had a central setting—a kind of out-of-phase pickup sound that Jeff couldn't get on his Les Paul, so I used mine for that sound.

It sounds exactly like a Les Paul.

Yeah—well, that's the amp and everything. You see, I could get a lot of tones out of the guitar that you normally couldn't. This confusion goes back to those early sessions again with the Les Paul. Those might not sound like a Les Paul, but that's what I used. It's just different amps, mic positions, and different things. Also, if you just crank it up to the distortion point so you can sustain notes, it's bound to sound like a Les Paul. I was using the Supro amp for the first album, and still do. The "Stairway to Heaven" solo was done when I pulled out the Telecaster—which I hadn't used for a long time—plugged it into the Supro, and away it went again. That's a different sound entirely from any of the rest of the first album. It was a good versatile setup.

> 66 My vocation is more in composition than in anything else. Building up harmonies, orchestrating the guitar like an army—a guitar army. 99

Do you just use your fingers when playing acoustic?

Yes. I used fingerpicks once, but I find them too spiky. They're too sharp. You can't get the tone or response that you would get, say, the way classical players approach gut-string instruments. The way they pick, the whole thing is the tonal response of the string. It seems important.

Can you describe your picking style?

I don't know, really. It's a cross between fingerstyle and flatpicking. There's a guy in England called Davey Graham, and he never used any fingerpicks or anything. He used a thumbpick every now and again, but I prefer just a flatpick and fingers, because then it's easier to get around from guitar to guitar. Well, it is for me, anyway. But, apparently, he has calluses on the left hand, and all over the right, as well. He can get so much attack on his strings, and he's really good.

The guitar on "Communication Breakdown" sounds as if it's coming out of a little shoebox.

Yeah. I put it in a small room—a little, tiny vocal booth–type thing—and miked it from a distance. You see, there's a very old recording maxim that goes: "Distance makes depth." I've used that recording technique a hell of a lot with the band. You're always used to them close-miking amps—just putting the microphone in front—but I'd have a mic right out the back as well, and then balance the two, getting rid of all the phasing problems. You shouldn't have to use EQ in the studio if the instruments sound right. It should all be done with the microphones. But everyone has gotten so carried away with EQ that they have forgotten the whole science of microphone placement. There aren't too many guys who know it. I'm sure Les Paul knows a lot. Obviously, he must have been well into that—as were all those who produced early rock records where there were only one or two mics in the studio.

The solo on "I Can't Quit You Babe" is interesting. There are many pull-offs in a sort of sloppy, but amazingly inventive style.

There are mistakes in it, but it doesn't make any difference. I'll always leave the mistakes in. I can't help it. The timing bits on the *A* and *B♭* parts are right, though it might sound wrong. The timing just *sounds* off. But there are some wrong notes. You've got to be reasonably honest about it.

Jumping ahead to *Led Zeppelin II*, the riff in the middle of "Whole Lotta Love" is a very composed and structured phrase.

"DY-NO-MITE" DISCS!

Led Zeppelin III, Led Zeppelin, 1970

Led Zeppelin IV, Led Zeppelin, 1971

Houses of the Holy, Led Zeppelin, 1973

I had it worked out already—that one—before entering the studio. I had rehearsed it. And then all that other stuff—sonic wave sounds and all that—I built up in the studio using effects and things. Treatments.

How is that descending riff done?

With a metal slide and backwards echo. I think I came up with that before anybody. I know it has been used a lot now, but not at the time. I thought of it on this Mickie Most thing. In fact, some of the things that might sound a bit odd have, in fact, backwards echo involved in them, as well.

Is the rest of the band in the studio when you put down the solos?

No. Never. I don't like anybody else in the studio when I'm putting on the guitar parts. I usually just limber up for a while, and then maybe do three solos, and take the best of the three.

You think your playing on the fourth LP is the best you've ever done?

Without a doubt. As far as consistency goes, and as far as the quality of playing on a whole album, I would say "yes." But I don't know what the best solo I've ever done is. I have no idea. My vocation is more in composition than in anything else. Building up harmonies, orchestrating the guitar like an army—a guitar army. I think that's where it's at, really, for me. I'm talking about actual orchestration in the same way you'd orchestrate a classical piece of music. Instead of using brass and violins, you treat the guitars with synthesizers or other devices—give them different treatments so that they have enough frequency range and scope and everything to keep the listener as totally committed to it as the player is. It's a difficult project, but it's one I've got to do.

The Queen of the
Slide Guitar—
Bonnie Raitt. (PETER
SIMON/RETNA LTD.)

BY PATRICIA BRODY

MAY 1977

Bonnie Raitt

BONNIE RAITT WAS ALMOST A FOLKSINGER—
part of the plethora of guitar-playing protesters of
the '60s led by Bob Dylan and Joan Baez. Sitting in her
girlhood bedroom in a house atop Coldwater Canyon's
peacefully affluent Mulholland Drive, Bonnie, born in
Burbank, California, in 1949, was inspired by loneliness
to teach herself guitar.

"If I'd been able to hang out with other kids, I'd
never have gotten into it," says the daughter of successful Broadway actor John Raitt, best known for his leading roles in musical comedies like *Pajama Game*,
Oklahoma!, and *Carousel*.

The Raitt house—last stop on the school bus
route—was somewhat isolated and not particularly con-
ducive to visits with friends. It hardly seemed located
within earshot of the whiney, mournful tones of a generation of blues guitarists whose techniques and repertoire
Bonnie came to adopt. Blues developed far from what
Raitt describes as the Los Angeles
"blonde-streaked surf scene" whose
"political and intellectual vacancy"
drove her to a progressive Quaker
boarding school in upstate New York.
There, feeling more in her element
among, as she calls them, "the preco-
cious children of leftist lawyers and

actors into modern theater of the absurd and Marxism," Raitt listened to Pete Seeger records, and expressed her own discontent playing Peter, Paul, and Mary and Kingston Trio–type laments on her guitar.

"For years," she recalls, "I wanted desperately to get old enough to be able to go to civil rights demonstrations and peace marches, be a beatnik, grow my hair, and have cheek bones like Joan Baez."

Encouraged in a musical home where "my mother was my father's accompanist, and we'd all sit around singing together," plus five years of piano lessons, Bonnie first turned to guitar—a Stella given to her as a Christmas present by her parents and grandparents—at the age of ten. She enthusiastically pursued her hobby through several summers at a camp in Massachusetts, where her counselors inspired even more longing for contact with the outside world with their exciting reports of musical events at the nearby Newport jazz and folk festivals.

Then, an album, *Blues at Newport '63*, containing tracks by John Lee Hooker, John Hammond, Mississippi John Hurt, as well as several other blues and folk artists, fell on Raitt's 14-year-old ears with enough impact to permanently change the direction of her music.

"From that point on," she remembers, "I was split into two parts. One side of me was all Joan Baez—my early idol—while the other suddenly had to learn whatever the hell it was Mississippi John Hurt was doing on 'Candy Man.'"

Acceptance to Radcliffe College in Cambridge, Massachusetts—they didn't have curfews there—further assured Raitt's entanglement with the blues. She soon came into contact with a leading figure of what she terms the "blues mafia," Dick Waterman. Waterman—a manager and promoter for many blues artists—seems to have been the catalyst who turned Bonnie's guitar hobby into a pursuit of somewhat greater intensity.

Cambridge, Massachusetts, was a turning point for you. What happened there?

I went there to go to college. I just played guitar as a hobby, but I ran into a lot of blues freaks at the Harvard station, WHRB, and at Club 47 in Harvard Square—a major outlet for musicians like Buddy Guy, Junior Wells, Taj Mahal, John Hurt, Skip James, and Canned Heat. Strangely enough, I'd rushed to get old enough to catch this great Greenwich Village folk scene I'd heard about, and, naturally, the year I moved to Cambridge, the club closed, and along came acid rock. This whole incredible political scene went to pot, literally, but that's when I met Dick Waterman.

By coincidence?

No. I was already a blues freak when I left California. There was a kind of blues mafia between New York, Philadelphia, and Cambridge—all these esoteric people talking about their blues idols' eating habits, and the obscure 78s they'd find—and Dick was a kind of a liaison. But he was unique in his concern for taking care of artists who were still alive, rather than trying to revive an era that was dead. Everyone at the Harvard station knew him, and if you wanted to do a blues show, you'd call Dick Waterman. Periodically, Son House, Skip James, or Arthur Crudup would come to town. Anyway, one afternoon a friend of mine invited me to this apartment on Franklin Street, and who was there housesitting for Dick Waterman, but Son House. I was just floored. Then, I began to meet them all.

> It could get easier if there were more women instrumentalists just sort of sprinkled around in more bands—and I don't mean the all-girl band situation.

All through Waterman?

At the time, Dick managed Junior Wells, Buddy Guy, Magic Sam, Otis Rush, Luther Allison, and J. B. Hutto, as well as many other traditional bluesmen. The reason it made sense to have so many artists under one agency was to protect them from the abuse of white blues promoters. Club owners would play one bluesman against the other. They'd say, "Well, we can get Bukka White for $200 less, so why bother with Son House?" Then Son's manager would have to drop his price in order to get the guy a gig at all. Dick was outraged, and by keeping them all under one agency, he could protect their rights. "You're not going to get any of them to play unless you pay what they deserve," he'd say. I started traveling around with Dick, driving Son, Skip, or Sleepy John Estes to the blues festivals, and I became real tight with them. These musicians came in, heard me trying to sound just like them, and they'd be flattered and helpful. If I'd been a young guy, they might have felt a bit threatened. I wasn't playing as good as them, but they were real tickled that I was into their style.

How did you develop your own style out of the traditional blues?

My style is probably the result of a problem. My voice—which is actually soprano—is around five keys up from where Robert Johnson or Son House would do a song, say, in Spanish open-G tuning. I can't tune the strings up or down to get that open octave. I have to capo up three or five frets to get the same tuning, which is the only way to make the guitar part sound good. You lose the octaves—with no cutaway you can't get your hand up there—and you've got only around three frets left to play slide. My National has a new, hybrid neck with 14 frets, and that's one of the reasons I went to electric—for the longer neck. Just adding my voice to a Fred McDowell guitar part would bring about a unique style, though.

What do you use for a slide?

Originally, I just broke off a wine bottle. Well, the style was called bottleneck, so I figured that's what it was. The only problem was you couldn't get wine bottles too easily if you didn't drink, and, at boarding school, there weren't a whole lot of wine-drinking orgies! Today, I still make them out of wine bottles—relatively cheap red wine. I flipped the bird a lot when I was a kid in California, so I knew how to isolate my middle finger, and I just naturally put that to use. Fred McDowell made his slides from Gordon's gin bottles, and they were only about 1 1/2" inches big. He'd have it on his little finger, and move his hand around a lot, like a violinist. My slide goes all the way from the second knuckle to the top of my finger, and my hands are smaller than his, so I can get a whole chord easier. I use the palm of my right hand to kind of muffle the sound when I pick with my thumb, and I use my thumb to get that thumpy kind of bass. I also use all three fingers when I pick. I sort of precariously balance my slide, so the middle finger wasn't the best choice, because when you go for a chord you have to learn how to keep the bottleneck from falling off.

You said before your tunings are somewhat limited . . .

I usually use open G [D, G, D, G, B, D, low to high] or A [E, A, C♯, E, A, E, low to high] for slide, and I move the capo up three frets, because most of the songs were in C. I have trouble with the capo, because I move around so much during the show that I need one you can slide around easy that doesn't bend the strings.

You use a Stratocaster for your electric slide playing?

Yes. All the people whose playing I love use Strats—John Hall, Lowell George, and Ry Cooder. But I use a Gibson for lead parts, because my Strat is set up just for slide with the action raised.

What about your amp?

Recently, I got a Music Man 212. It's real nice because it has a built-in preamp.

What strings and other accessories do you use?

When we were on the road together, Lowell [George] gave me one of those MXR compressors, and it has given me a whole new scope of sound. It has made me work harder to find my own blend. Besides the compressor, I have an MXR phaser—which I sometimes like to play an acoustic guitar through—and an MXR Noise Gate. I could just as easily be playing through a Pignose or something—I don't really care. But this combination—the Music Man with those three pedals—seems to work out best onstage.

For the Strat, I use Darco strings, gauged .013, .016, .022, .036, .044, .056. On the Gibson, it's medium-gauge Sonomatics with an unwound third string, gauged .020. On the acoustics, it's medium- or heavy-gauge strings—usually D'Merles.

The main thing about my style is fingerpicking, so I don't have a flatpick. I use clear plastic Dobra fingerpicks. When on the road, if I lose my pick bag—which is really a little cosmetic case where I keep my two capos and all my picks—it's really hard to replace them. When I do find thumbpicks and fingerpicks that fit, I buy about 300. Well, at least a whole bunch.

Many female musicians express so much frustration and resentment regarding their difficulties in breaking into—or coping with—the music business. Have you run into this?

It's a terrible problem. It hasn't hindered me so much, but I hear about it all the

"DY-NO-MITE" DISCS!

Give It Up, 1972

Streetlights, 1974

The Glow, 1979

time. You know, it's hard for guys to break in, too. There are just too many musicians around—especially guitarists. It could get easier if there were more women instrumentalists just sort of sprinkled around in more bands—and I don't mean the all-girl band situation.

Can you think of any way that you, as a woman musician who has made a breakthrough, can help?

What's so hard is that women aren't heard enough to be in the position to be hired. I won't fire a member of my band to bring in a woman, but if I needed a replacement, and I heard a woman who was great, I'd love to hire her. Unfortunately, my music isn't established enough, but I hope in the next year or so to do something to try to help. Maybe start a record label, or create a special auditioning outlet for women.

I was lucky. I played the guitar—which seemed like a gimmick. And one of the reasons I got to where I am is because I was cheap. Because when you hired me as an opening act, you didn't have to hire a whole band, you just hired me, and then you only had to pay one person. I carried my own guitar, and I did a little blues and some ballads. And I didn't threaten the male act on the bill!

Glam-guitar hero
Mick Ronson. (CHRIS
FOSTER/RETNA UK)

BY STEVE ROSEN

DECEMBER 1976

Mick Ronson

THE THREE-WORD TITLE OF MICK RONSON'S second solo album also happens to accurately describe his approach to the guitar: *Play, Don't Worry*. At nearly 30, British-born Mick likes to perform music that challenges his skills as a guitar player, keyboardist, arranger, and producer. He claims not to be particularly concerned with audience reaction to either his choice of band or the type of music he decides to play. Perhaps this attitude accounts for his most recent stint with Bob Dylan's Rolling Thunder Revue, a folk-oriented band most people would not associate with Ronson's more widely known electric style, best demonstrated earlier in his career with David Bowie and the Spiders from Mars.

It has taken years for Mick to develop his flexibility. At age three, he began playing an accordion given to him by a next-door neighbor. He remembers hearing his first "real piece of music" when he went to see a Charlie Chaplin film called *Limelight*. The movie inspired him to return to the accordion with a fervor that so impressed his parents they offered him piano lessons. The fledgling musician's talents were thwarted, however, by various teachers' inabilities to cope with so young an artist. When he reached 11 years of age, he experimented with both violin and recorder,

and found that the string instrument really sparked his interest.

"Violin was quite fun," Mick remarks, "but after about three years, I got fed up with it, because people used to make fun of you if you carried a violin case. All the big lads were getting motorbikes, and I wanted to go out into the streets and into bowling alleys and things. I used to pay people to carry my violin because I was afraid to—there were some tough lads there."

Childish ridicule coupled with an insensitive teacher ("He used to rap my knuckles all the time") led to such discouragement that Mick not only dropped his pursuit of the violin, but left music entirely for three years. Then, when he was 17, he bought a Rossetti acoustic guitar for £14, and soon after joined a local band.

"I think that was the best time ever," Ronson reflects on the early stages of his career. "Just learning how to play. It was a real thrill simply to switch on an amplifier and listen to it work. One of the amps had an echo chamber, and it was just amazing—all these sounds coming out!"

The band stayed together for about nine months, and succeeded in landing a couple of jobs. Initially without a bass player, when one was finally obtained, the time seemed right to switch to larger amps into which the microphones, guitars, and bass were plugged.

"I don't know what it sounded like out front," he remarks, "but onstage it was awful."

Ronson spent time in various bands—with names like the Cresters and the Rats—but not until he ventured south to London, from Hull in Yorkshire, for the second time (the first such jaunt left him hungry and penniless) did he finally meet David Bowie.

"He wanted to put a band together, and I happened to be there," explains Mick.

In his first years with Bowie, Ronson used small Fender amps—both in the studio and onstage—but during Bowie's Ziggy Stardust days, the guitarist switched to Marshalls.

"That's when it started getting noisy," he comments.

On *The Rise and Fall of Ziggy Stardust*, he used a 100-watt top with one bottom. Unlike most guitar players, Mick didn't seem highly concerned about the particular brand of amplifier or guitar he used.

"Often, I wouldn't even think of what I was plugging into," he says. "Sometimes, it doesn't matter to me at all, as long as it works. I don't really have a preference for one amp over another."

Currently, he plays through a Fender Pro Reverb, and, in the studio, he switches to a Marshall 100-watt stack.

A Telecaster was the first "really playable guitar" he owned (at age 19), but he changed later to a 1958 Gibson Les Paul Custom used throughout his Bowie period. He played the Les Paul in its unaltered state with Bowie, Ian Hunter, Mott the Hoople, and, most recently, with Dylan and the Rolling Thunder Revue. Mick also has two other Les Paul Customs, but both are reported to be in various states of disrepair. His feeling about strings and picks still runs parallel to his attitude toward amplifiers—whatever is available will suffice. He once used heavy picks for both electric and acoustic playing, but found the flexibility of a light plectrum better for smoother and livelier rhythms on acoustic. Otherwise, he claims, "If it's hard enough" any pick satisfies him. His string arrangement changes occasionally, but he usually returns to a Rotosound setup, gauged .009, .011, .015, .026, .038, and .046. He expresses little concern for pedals, although he has employed a fuzz box and a wah-wah with the Bowie band, and a phase shifter for studio work.

The guitarist's lack of passion about the tools of his trade in no way reflects his attitude toward playing. His interaction with the Revue greatly stimulated his blues-rock roots. He has been learning the intricacies of a more country-flavored style, as well as finding other new things to try, and confides, "I want to be able to play better than anyone else can."

He admits that he does not know what scales he draws from, but rather uses "the same runs all the time." He feels a reawakened interest in experimenting—a desire he believes was stifled by the Bowie group.

"I'd never bring a guitar around to play," Mick recalls.

"DY-NO-MITE" DISCS!

Ziggy Stardust, **David Bowie,** 1972

Aladdin Sane, **David Bowie,** 1973

Slaughter on 10th Avenue, 1974

"I'd only play it when I was in the studio or onstage. It started becoming secondary to other things I wanted to do—producing, arranging, or whatever. I should have played more than I did, but I used to have to force myself to take it out—which is a real strange way for a guitar player to be!

"I remember playing on the road once with a guitar that had a cracked neck, and we got gaffer's tape to fix the thing up. So there I was onstage playing this axe with gaffer's tape. I don't know how the hell I did it. If something went wrong with the guitar, I'd just ignore it. I'd sort of bash it about a bit, tune it up, and never bother with much more than that. I don't know what made me be like that, but now that I'm getting deeply into guitar playing again, I find that it's really getting to me. Now, it's a real pleasure to pick up a good instrument, and I'm getting the hots for getting some fine guitars—the kind I have to put away carefully."

From his earliest association with David Bowie, to his work with Mott the Hoople, and finally to his affiliation with Dylan and Roger McGuinn (Mick played several instruments on, and produced McGuinn's *Cardiff Rose*), Mick Ronson has maintained a bold and solid playing technique. He doesn't look back to see what people might say about his varied musical career.

"It doesn't matter what the public thinks about my playing," he states firmly, "whether it's Dylan or anybody—as long as I'm enjoying myself. Some people will probably think to themselves, 'Why is he playing that hillbilly stuff? Why doesn't he just go back to what he was doing?' And that *is* a good thing to do now and again—it's always good if you can keep up what you've done in the past, as well as develop yourself in the present. You never know when you'll want to use what you've learned before sometime in the future. Of course, I hope everyone will like my music, but, either way, I have to keep moving on."

Carlos Santana
divines inspiration
with a Gibson SG.
(CHIRS FOSTER/
RETNA UK)

BY DAN FORTE

JUNE 1978

Carlos Santana

TENOR SAXOPHONIST JOHN COLTRANE, ONE OF modern jazz's true innovators, once said, "We are always searching. I think that now we are at the point of finding." Devadip Carlos Santana, like Coltrane, is a searcher—or, as he puts it, a seeker. The similarities between the two artists don't stop there. As with Coltrane's music, Santana's music has reflected the spiritual lifestyle he has chosen. Like Coltrane, he is an innovator, and, above all, an individual voice on his instrument, the guitar.

John Coltrane was a major inspiration for Carlos, so the parallels are no doubt more than coincidence. The title tune of the Santana band's seventh album, *Welcome*, was a Coltrane composition. At one stage, Devadip would even sleep with a tape of Coltrane music playing all night long.

But Santana was wise enough to know that there could only be one John Coltrane, and he listened to the music for inspiration—not to cop lines or even stylistic modes. Carlos Santana is such an individualist that it's difficult to hear direct traces of the musicians he cites as influences, except on rare occasions. He will talk for hours about his deep love for the blues, rattling off an endless list of

favorite performers of the genre. Yet in his ten albums with the Santana band and his various sole projects, he has never recorded a blues tune—at least not in standard blues form. The blues, like the other factors that make up Santana's sound, is reflected as a feeling—not as notes or rhythms.

To this day, the name Santana brings to mind a picture of a battery of Latin percussionists behind their leader, who leans backwards, eyes clenched shut in concentration, as he squeezes the notes from his guitar. The Santana band was the first group to successfully blend Latin and Afro rhythms with rock music. Originally known as the Santana Blues Band—later shortened to its leader's surname—the group built a strong following at Bill Graham's Fillmore Auditorium in San Francisco. The young band received national acclaim, thanks to the Woodstock festival in 1969, the same year their first LP, *Santana*, debuted. *Santana* produced two hit singles in "Jingo" and "Evil Ways," and turned platinum within a year—an achievement few groups of that period could claim.

> **It's a cry. It's a crying melody. That's mostly what I hear, and then I have to find the chords.**

More hit albums and singles followed—despite numerous personnel changes in the group. The Santana band's direction changed as did its guitarist/leader's ideals. By the group's fourth album, *Caravanserai*, artists such as Coltrane, Charles Lloyd, McCoy Tyner, Thelonious Monk, Miles Davis, and the group Weather Report provided the inspiration that had previously come from B. B. King, Jimmy Reed, and others.

What Carlos was searching for, musically and personally, he found in Sri Chinmoy, his spiritual guru. Santana was introduced to Sri Chinmoy by electrifying guitarist Mahavishnu John McLaughlin. The two artists joined forces on *Love Devotion Surrender* in 1973, which was as much a religious statement as it was a musical one.

But the more Santana's music began to mirror the tranquility and inner peace Devadip had found, the less it sounded like the energetic, feverish group that had insured "street music's" inclusion in the list of psychedelic San Francisco rock outfits. Carlos began to realize that the concert-opening moments of silent meditation—and the extended improvisational excursions—were alienating some of his old fans. People wanted to move and dance.

While on tour with McLaughlin in 1973, Santana dropped by a Seattle beer bar to jam with one of his early, pre-guru inspirations, Elvin Bishop. The ex–Butterfield Blues Band guitarist's brand of ham-and-eggs rock and blues—and the crowd's involvement with it—brought Carlos to the realization that "the highest form of spirituality is joy. If you don't have that, man, then I don't care for spirituality."

When you were growing up, did your father play in mariachi bands? Did he teach you things?

Yes. I started playing the violin first. I was playing Beethoven's "Minuet in *G*" and "Poet and Peasant Overture" by von Suppé—you know, classical songs. But I hated the violin. I just hated the sound of it, and the smell of it. And, to me, anything I played on the violin sounded like Jack Benny when he was fooling around [*laughs*]. Later, I saw this band in Tijuana, where I grew up, and they were totally imitating B. B. King, Ray Charles, Bobby Bland, and Little Richard. I said, "Oh, man! This is the stuff I want to get into." I was about 11 or so, and it was the first blues I'd heard. I never felt empathy with Mexican music. Not that I hated it—I just couldn't relate to it. I usually equated Mexican music with drunk Mexicans having a brawl, and overemphasizing the macho trips, so I really couldn't get into it. I grew up with that environment. I could get into the blues more. It was more natural to me.

When you moved to San Francisco, did you eventually get into the white blues movement that was happening at that time?

Paul Butterfield? Yeah, he was the one who started the whole thing for a lot of people. See, when I came to America, my American friends would be listening to the Dave Clark Five and the Beach Boys, and I couldn't stand that. I'd say, "Why are you into these guys? They aren't even saying nothing, man. Listen to Ray Charles and Bobby Bland." And they'd say, "That stuff is old." And all of a sudden, two things hit me: One was seeing Paul Butterfield and Muddy Waters, and the other was Cream's first record [*Fresh Cream*]. It just totally turned me around. I said, "How can these guys play blues like that?"

That's when I started to play hookey from Mission High. Stan Marcum, who subsequently became my first manager, took me to Winterland to see Paul Butterfield and Muddy Waters when Muddy had Little Walter on harp. Man, I was knocked out for weeks. I was in a daze. I couldn't believe what blues could do to people. I could see people's eyes and faces and the way they were reacting when the band was playing the blues. I could see that the group was feeding these people, and they were feeding me. It was one of the most fantastic concerts I've ever been to.

Did the original Santana Blues Band play blues standards?

We did songs by B. B. King, Ray Charles—like "Woke Up This Morning" and "Mary Ann"—and we would do our own versions of the first two Butterfield albums. That's when I started getting into drugs. Drugs don't fit me now, but if I hadn't ever taken them I'd probably be kind of square and more prejudiced. I don't think I would have been as open to things like [jazz flautist] Charles Lloyd and [saxophonist] John Handy. It can make you receptive and sensitive to a certain level, right? The Beatles, Cream, and the Yardbirds were all doing it, so you say, "Gee, maybe there's something to it."

Did the Latin influences creep into the Santana band because of the things you'd heard as a kid, or did an outside musician bring that element to the band?

[*Long pause.*] It took me a long time, just now, to remember when the congas came in. We were exclusively a blues band at first. People ask me a lot of times how the change took place, and I think the reason was that we'd go around "Hippy Hill" and Aquatic Park in San Francisco, and they used to have congas and wine, and that's where we got the congas in the band. Somebody brought this conga player to jam with us, and he threw us into a whole different thing. Actually, we never play "Latin music"—you know, it's a crossover. I just play whatever I hear.

Did you originally plan to add a conga player, yet continue playing blues?

Yeah. Even when we had a conga player it was still the Santana Blues Band. Later we got Chepito [Areas], and he was playing congas and timbales. Then, we dropped the "Blues Band" and started to play more of a crossover. And we were listening to Miles and the Jazz Crusaders. After that, it was really interesting, because even Chicago came out with congas. Actually, Harvey Mandel was probably the first guy to put congas on a rock and roll album [*Cristo Redentor*]. I saw him and Charlie Musselwhite [as the Southside Sound System] at the Avalon one time, and they played "Cristo Redentor" and "Wade in the Water," and I was knocked out. I learned a lot from them.

I really admire guys like Harvey Mandel whose sound I can identify, because it takes a lot of work. Nobody can say that you are born with it. You work for it, and carve your own individuality. In fact, if people want to find out how to develop this, a good way is to get a tape recorder, and for half an hour, turn out the lights in your house and get into a room that's kind of dark—where you don't have interruptions. Then, just play with a rhythm machine. After a while, it's like a deck of cards on the table, and you can begin to see the riffs that came from this guy, the riffs that came from that guy, and then the two or three riffs that are yours. Then, you start concentrating on yours, and, to me, that's how you develop your own individual sound. You play a couple of notes and say, "Gee, that sounds like Eric Clapton" or "That sounds like George Benson." But then you play two or three notes, and say, "Man, that's me."

When you hear an idea for a song in your head, is it usually a melody or a set of changes or a rhythmic motif or what?

It's a cry. It's a crying melody. That's mostly what I hear, and then I have to find the chords. Sometimes, it's the other way around, and one chord could almost make up for three melodies. But, sometimes, the melody is so clear, you want to find three passing chords for that melody.

Your guitar solos seem to stay pretty close to the melody of the song itself, as opposed to players like, say, Al Di Meola or John McLaughlin, who use a lot of scalar things. Are you thinking of the song's basic theme throughout your solo?

Yes. To me, the heart of the song is the melody. And I approach the melody from a singer's point of view—a simple singer, not a singer who scats a lot like George Benson. If you'll notice, a lot of guitar players riff like horn players. And I don't really like guitar players like that. Not that I dislike them with a passion, but it doesn't appeal to me—it's boring. I think more like a layman singing [*sings*], "Lovely Rita, meter maid . . ." You don't care what chords are underneath—it's the basic feeling of the song that gets you immediately. As far as I'm concerned, the point of music is to tell stories with a melody. All that stuff about playing notes, to me, is just like watching some cat pick up weights. After a while, who wants to see somebody flex their muscles?

Did the collaboration with John McLaughlin come about because you were both involved with Sri Chinmoy?

I was a seeker, and I still am a seeker. Even music is secondary to me—as much as I love it. Mahavishnu called me and said they wanted to know if we could do this album together, and he also wanted to know if I was interested in coming to see Sri Chinmoy. He felt that I was aspiring or crying for another kind of awareness, because, at that time, I had already made a commitment to close the book on drugs and booze and that kind of stuff. I started reading books about India and about spiritual masters, and it inspired me to work harder. Some people call it ambition, but I call it inspiration. When you have that, it's like having a different kind of energy—pure energy—a different kind of fuel. Sometimes, it's totally in this center of creativity, and it just flows through you, and, all of a sudden, you don't have to worry about who's going to like or dislike it. When it's over, you feel just like a bee. You don't know why you did it, but, all of a sudden, you've accumulated all this honey. So that's what brought us together. I did learn so much from him. He's an incredible musician.

Was your Yamaha electric built to your specifications?

Yeah. It's almost shaped like a Yamaha SG body, but it's really fat like a Les Paul. It has more frets, and for sustain I asked them to put a big chunk of metal like a grand piano right where the tailpiece is. You hit it, and it's like hitting an acoustic grand piano—it really resonates. When you hit the note, you don't have to use all those gadgets to sustain. In fact, I never use sustain pedals. Gadgets always make you sound like you're frying hamburgers through the amp.

When did you start using the Mesa/Boogie amp?

My brother Jorge turned me on to that. I was in New York, and I was really unhappy with my Fender Twins. It

"DY-NO-MITE" DISCS!

Abraxas, 1970

Santana III, 1971

Caravanserai, 1972

gave me headaches just to try to sustain. When Leo Fender left the company, he took something with him, because almost overnight I couldn't get sustain from the new Fenders. Jorge came over and said, "You got to try this amp." And it really looked like the Tubes' amplifiers. It had a snakeskin kind of cover—really cheesy looking [*laughs*]. But, man, it sustained like crazy, so I never gave it back to Jorge [*laughs*].

What type of strings are you using?

I use Yamaha strings—generally .008, .011, .014, .024, .032, and .042.

You've mentioned several artists as being crossovers, which is somewhat controversial, as some jazz purists no doubt resent a rocker like Jeff Beck winning this year's *Playboy* poll as Best Jazz Guitarist. In fact, the term "jazz" has been used to describe your playing.

And I'm not. I don't know why they classify certain artists like they do, but I'm not bothered by it, because I know that, first and foremost, I'm an instrument myself trying to play something back to you. I don't consider myself a guitar player as much as I am a seeker who wants to manifest his vision through that particular instrument. I consider a guitar player somebody who sounds like a guitar player. In this day and age, it's hard to tell who's *not* a crossover, except Keith Jarrett. I don't consider "crossover" to be a negative term. Some players have used it just to make more bread, and their heart isn't in it, and that's prostitution. I just play whatever is comfortable without offending or belittling my instrument or my own integrity.

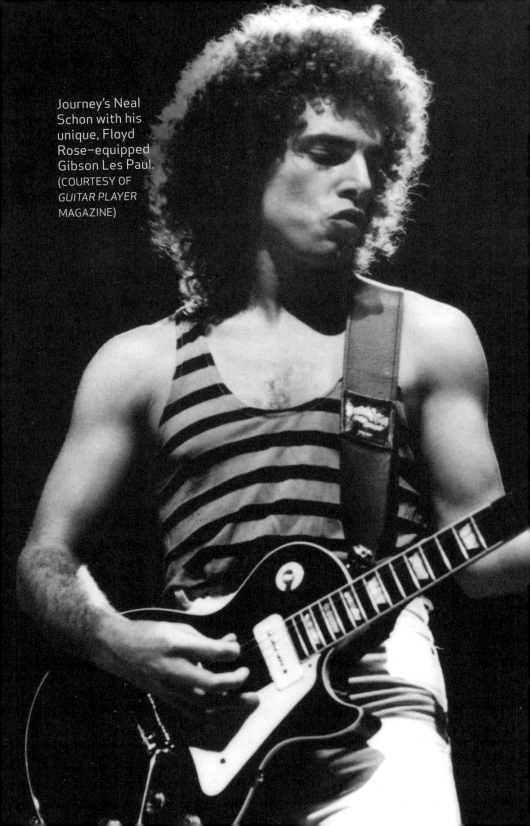

Journey's Neal Schon with his unique, Floyd Rose–equipped Gibson Les Paul. (COURTESY OF *GUITAR PLAYER* MAGAZINE)

BY JACK MCDONOUGH

MARCH 1976

Neal Schon

WHEN NEAL SCHON WAS 16, HE WAS PLAYING and touring with Santana—one of the biggest-selling bands of all time. He did that for three years, and cut three albums with them. Now, he is the central figure in a new band—Journey—that has already established a national reputation. Neal is 21 now.

The obvious question about Schon is, how did he get so good so young?

Well, like many other players who got very good while very young, he had two things going for him: He started at age ten, and he had a musician parent—his father Matt—who got him started, helped him along, and, most of all, provided Neal with an example of how to make one's living out of a love for playing.

His father, a woodwind player who does one-nighters at San Francisco hotels like the Fairmont and the Hilton and teaches music in San Mateo, California, had Neal playing piano when he was five. Neal took up the guitar at age ten, and later played oboe in his high school band.

"I could read music, and I learned theory," says Schon, "but it took me away from what I wanted to do, and what was natural for me to do. I can't do any of the theoretical stuff anymore. I could if I brushed up on it,

but I haven't had any reason to go back to it, because now things just flow out of me naturally."

In those early stages, Neal was pretty good on the oboe.

"I was first-chair oboe with my high-school concert band," he recalls. "I got to play all the solos, and there are a lot of oboe solos in concert music. I was getting that down until, one day, I dropped the oboe, and the whole thing went out of line. See, no two oboes are ever the same. You have to learn which notes are a little bit sharper or flatter, and compensate with your mouth. So after I dropped my oboe, it was like starting all over again. So I just went off to my guitar."

When he went off with the guitar, Neal brought along a few famous records.

"Cream and Hendrix had come out," Schon remembers, "and I heard these sounds corning out of a guitar that amazed me. So I decided to sit down with the records. I spent a couple of years sitting in my little room with a record player and my guitar, and I went over and over two albums: *Wheels of Fire* and *Are You Experienced? Wheels of Fire* blew me away. Clapton has been one of my main influences. I just studied the records so many times that I got to the point where I could play every one of his solos exactly like on the record—same fingering, same vibrato, same tone. I was also into fiddling around with the electronics, even though I didn't know anything about it. I'd add fuzz boxes and other components just to see what I'd come upon. I started using a preamp so I could get the right tone, and still play at a low enough volume to play with the records. That's real important—to have the same tone happening as the record you're listening to."

Schon's "first decent guitar"—the one he had while studying Clapton and Hendrix—was a Gibson ES-335. He later tried a Gibson Barney Kessel model ("I hated it"), and then a Les Paul Standard. He now has a Fender Telecaster with a humbucking pickup in front and a single-coil in back, which he considers "one of the best guitars I have for studio work." However, he still mostly uses a Les Paul.

"I did a couple of tricks with the pickups," Neal says. "But the guy who showed me made me promise I'd never pass along the tricks to anyone else."

With Santana, Neal used an old goldtop Les Paul with P-90 pickups, although now he prefers humbuckers. He still has the goldtop, but hasn't used it in the studio since he left Santana. For acoustic work, Schon uses a Guild.

With Santana, Neal always used Ernie Ball Super Slinky strings, gauged .008, .009, .011, .022, .030, .038.

"I can't play with those anymore," Schon says. "Now, I use Gibson Extra-Lights. They're not much heavier—.009, .010, .012, 022, .030, .038—but it's a big difference to me. They don't go dead so fast."

Neal has switched picks from the Santana days, when he used a Fender Light.

"They'd bust all the time," he explains, "so now I use a nylon Herco Light."

Neal says that in getting his sound he uses a lot of different things: "They're not all the same, and I don't use them all the time. I have about 20 amplifiers, and I use different ones for different things. For example, I have a Fender Super Six loaded with four 12" Celestion speakers, and three Fender rotary speakers, each carrying a 12" Altec speaker.

"I haven't found a top yet for the three rotary speakers," he says. "Until a while ago, I was only using two, and hooking them to the Super Six top with an extra Super Six top driving them. I'm looking for a top now—a tube amp of about 200 watts."

In addition, Neal uses a large Yamaha rotary speaker, a Vox wah-wah, a Roland Sustainer, an old gray Echoplex, a Fender Blender distortion box, and a Fender Deluxe Reverb for studio use (with 10" and 12" JBL speakers hooked out of phase).

Neal keeps the action about 1/4" off the fretboard at the twelfth fret.

"It's really low and light—really easy to play," he says. "I like to have the whole thing under the control of my fingers."

Schon's association with Santana began when he was playing at a Palo Alto, California club called the Poppycock with a local band. Santana members Gregg Rolie and Michael Shrieve—who knew the bass player in that band—came into the Poppycock one night and, as Neal tells it, "ended up jamming with us at the end of the evening. After that, I started hanging out with Gregg and going into the studio, and eventually I started playing with the band. I came in on the third LP, which was just called *Santana*, and I played on *Caravanserai*, and on *Live!*. It took me a while to get into the band, because my rhythm was so weak. I had been used to playing heavy rock and roll, and Santana's rhythms were difficult for me to do, at first. Then, after I locked into them, I more or less heard my own parts, and I added them to what was already there."

Though Clapton influenced him greatly, Schon states: "Hendrix was number one to me. In jazz, my favorite was Wes Montgomery. Technically, George Benson is great—he's all over the axe—but Montgomery was the *only* cat. He could play so many notes, but every note was as meaningful as one note. I also listened to Mike Bloomfield, B. B. King, Harvey Mandel, Peter Green, Jimmy Page, and Jeff Beck. When I didn't really have my own style, I'd come to a solo in Santana, and I'd take pieces from everyone of these guys, and stick them into one riff. I'd think to myself, 'It would sound hot if Beck were playing right there, doing some nasty thing, and then Clapton here, and Hendrix there. I was really into English music.'"

Neal spoke briefly about his departure from Santana: "When Carlos and I first got together, we were really tight, and we sounded that way on record. But after a while, it got to be like a battle on stage. It was a drag, so I decided to split. Gregg Rolie split at the same time. He went and opened a restaurant for a year."

Schon and Rolie eventually formed Journey at the prodding of Walter Herbert—better known as Herbie—who had done equipment work with Santana. It took quite a while for the band that was to be known as Journey to come together, but their first album, *Journey*, came out this spring, and the band went on the road.

"The people who have bought the album," says Neal, "aren't really kids. It's people 20 to 35, and a lot of the bands we've been performing with haven't been the right chemistry for us. We did a tour with [the] Hunter Ronson [Band], which stiffed. That's really not our audience. We played with Hot Tuna, and that's not the

"DY-NO-MITE" DISCS!

Journey, Journey, 1975

Infinity, Journey, 1978

Evolution, Journey, 1979

right chemistry, either. But if you can get the Hot Tuna diehards to listen to you, and turn them around in the middle of a set—which we did—then I figure we're accomplishing something."

Neal, who has been composing a lot on piano ("It's often a lot easier to hear things on piano and adapt to it"), has particular methods for working with the band.

"I don't like to practice that much—except when I have a brainstorm for a tune," he says. "Sometimes, I'll have three parts: one part for a solo, one melodic part for vocals, and a bridge that glues them together. I like to rehearse with the band, because that enables me to stick the parts together correctly. A lot of times, I can't hear the parts quite right myself. Then, the band grows as a whole. That's what I'm into now. I'm not interested in being the hottest or fastest guitarist around. There are a million guitar players now trying to be the hottest. That's what I was like when I was 16. I played with Elvin Bishop a lot— I was really into blues then—and I knew I was hot. You can call me conceited if you want, but I was playing rock and roll that I can't even play now. Every time I played, I'd get into a trance. My music is my total outlet for everything. If I couldn't play, I don't know what I'd do."

In the '70s, Pete Townshend powered the Who's onslaught with a number of Les Pauls. (COURTESY OF *GUITAR PLAYER* MAGAZINE)

BY MICHAEL BROOKS

MAY/JUNE 1972

Pete Townshend

CHIEF LICK-MAKER OF THE WHO IS PETE Townshend, whose influences have included John Lee Hooker, Steve Cropper, Jimi Hendrix, and the Yardbirds. He is acclaimed as the first guitarist to stack amplifiers, putting Marshall cabinets on one another, and also among the first to use feedback creatively. He is the epitome of stage presence with his long, lean figure seemingly jumping six feet in the air, and his wind-milling arm striking his guitar's strings with the effect of a lightning-clouded sky. The following interview with Peter took place at the St. Francis Hotel in San Francisco, between midnight and three AM, while the Who was on its recent American tour.

The Who plays very loud. How are your ears?

Not too good. I'm not really too unhappy about it, but I'm also kind of angry in a way. Rock stars are going to start going deaf a lot sooner than they think.

Have any of your instruments been modified?

I wouldn't touch the Les Paul—it's a 1953. I never got into old guitars until Joe Walsh rang me up one night, and said, "I've got something for you." We buy one another presents. He buys me concert amps, and I buy him synthesizers, and we have become very good friends. Anyway, I

said "What?" He said, "A 1957 Gretsch." I opened the case, and it was bright orange, and I thought, "Ugh! It's horrible. I hate it." I was being polite, so I took it home, went into my studio, plugged it in, and it totally wrecked me. It's the best guitar I've got now. I used that guitar on every track on *Who's Next*. It's the finest guitar I've ever owned, and it's the loudest guitar I've ever owned. Man, it whips any pickup I've ever come across. It won't stay in tune on stage, but if it did, I would use it.

What about the Gibson SG?

Well, the SG story is a bit disappointing. The first time I started to use the Gibson SG is when I got fed up with Fenders, because they were too clean. But I liked them because they were tough. In my guitar-smashing days, the Fender would last two or three shows if I wanted to smash it up. But I was into Jimi Hendrix, and if I wanted a dirty tone, I'd have to use a fuzz box. So I went to our manager and said I really need an alternative to this, and thought I'd like the SG. I played it, and it sang to me, and I've used SGs ever since. I don't break them deliberately any more, but when I've had a few drinks, I bang them, and they crack and break. They're made out of a really light wood, so I can bend the neck back to get vibrato effects. But the Gibson factory stopped making those particular SGs about a year ago, so we said, "You're going to have to make them for us." They said, "Okay, but it's going to be about $300 a guitar." So we had four of them made for the beginning of the tour, but the guitars were totally different. The pickups were in a different position, and on and on, so we said, "Forget it." Then, I raided every music store in the country looking for old SG's. I'm using a natural wood SG for this tour—it's not modified, except for a Tune-o-matic bridge—and the one I use on "Baby Don't You Do It" is a 1966 SG Standard. But my favorite guitar now for the stage is the Les Paul Deluxe with mini humbuckers—they're really loud.

> " Ego-wise, I'm musically happiest when I feel like I'm driving everyone else to do good things— when I'm not being the pin man. "

For your string setup, I imagine have a heavier gauge on the bottom strings and a lighter on the top ones because of your combination of lead and rhythm playing?

No—that's the setup you get when you buy a regular-gauge Sonomatic set. I use a heavy set that's [high to low] .022, .028, .028, .032, .044, .056. If I'm going to hit a note or bend it, I really want to have to struggle for it. Because I'm so physically wound up on the stage, if I wanted to, I could pull the string up and break it with my hand. It's really weird. When I'm in the dressing room playing, I can hardly stretch the strings, and then when I go on stage, I get a buzz and those heavy strings feel really slinky.

The first guy that I met—my idol in England—was Mick Green, who used to play with Johnny Kidd and the Pirates. He was the first big note-bender, particularly on the G string. And you'd freak over Jimmy Burton, and you'd freak over Mickey Green, and you'd wonder how they got that sound. So I got to see Mickey play, and I went back-stage to see him, and I asked if I could play his guitar. He said, "Sure, man." I picked it up, and he has strings like bloody piano strings—they're huge! And the G string isn't plain—it's wound, and he used to stretch it practically to the A string and beyond. Big hands, and he would pull it down and tuck it under, as well. That's what really buzzed me out—using the heavy strings—because a lot of younger guitarists tend to get light strings, and they quickly get into bending riffs, and all those Jeff Beck trips. But it's like the string, the fretboard, and the pick-up doing are doing the work, and you're just piddling about. When Freddie King—who is my man at the moment—does a bend, he's pulling it a good inch to get that sound, and he works for it. If you're going to hit a note, you've got to work for it. Leslie West—who is another amazing guitarist—gave me an old Les Paul Junior once, and it was strung the way he uses it, and those strings were just a bit lighter than what I use.

How much of your leads are improvised?

Well, in the loose bits, it's off the cuff. Sometimes, when an audience is passive, we freak and say, "For Christ's sake get up off your ass and do something." Then, a lot of things will come out that don't ordinarily come out.

How important is the music over the acrobatics in a typical Who performance?

It's really hard to explain, but I can't separate the music and the act any more. From the very beginning, my favorite quote I've ever said in an interview was, "We never let the music get in the way of our stage act." I mean, in a lot of ways that's true, because "stage act" means we are committed to one another and the audience, and "music" means we are committed to the way we play. It means that we are committed to our limitations. You know, if there's something on the guitar I want to do, and I can't do it, I'm going to be frustrated.

When you are actually playing a lead, is it out of scales, chords, patterns, or what?

Well, I started out as a rhythm player, and a few of my lead licks are things I developed in recording sessions. I don't think I even approach being a lead player. I'm very much part of a band and a riff maker. I enjoy backing people up, and letting people ride on top. I guess what I'm saying is that I make a good audience. Ego-wise, I'm musically happiest when I feel like I'm driving everyone else to do good things—when I'm not being the pin man. That is, to me, quite a bit more important.

As for solos, I was happiest listening to Jimi Hendrix—that was like heaven. For me, it was probably a good thing he died, because it made me realize that I wasn't going to be at any more Jimi Hendrix concerts, and that I was going to have to try and do it for myself again. I wish I could play like that. I mean, I enjoy being white and stiff, but there are moments when I would really like to just fly like Hendrix or Charlie Parker. To transcend the instrument, and transcend the audience, until the music itself becomes a hymn.

On that note, what role did *Tommy* play in your development as a group?

Tommy did something very strange. It showed us that it is possible to do something in rock on a grand scale, and still allow it to be rock.

What about your musical objectives?

"DY-NO-MITE" DISCS!

Live at Leeds, the Who, 1970

Who's Next, the Who, 1971

Quadrophenia, the Who, 1973

I think the biggest, really, is to hit on a solid, celestial music buzz. Heavenly music. Music I would imagine you'd hear in heaven.

Your tie-in to the celestial really amazes me, as rock appears to be a more physical means of enlightenment.

Right. Rock and roll is so much more physical, and that's what is so great about it. I don't like to see rock and roll abused. I don't like to see it used as a pawn in some political argument, or as some freak's weapon. It does what it does, because it is what it is. Rock and roll is about going to a hall, seeing a group you dig, and, for maybe a good half hour, forgetting about life, forgetting about your hang-ups, and even forgetting the fact you've paid to see some superstars. Suddenly, you even forget that you're there—you're just hearing some music. That's a spiritual thing, and rock and roll is spiritual in a different way. It makes people like come together and be equal. It makes people become selfless. It makes them forget themselves.

Robin Trower's
moody Stratocaster
lines often reached
near-cinematic
heights. (COURTESY
OF *GUITAR PLAYER*
MAGAZINE)

BY STEVE ROSEN

APRIL 1974

Robin Trower

ROBIN TROWER'S STRETCH IN PROCOL HARUM was like putting a polar bear in the Sahara Desert. While Procol was dabbling in classical forms with droning organs and mystical lyrics, Robin was diving into the mystique of Jimi Hendrix, and writing moving ballads like "Song for a Dreamer." Although the band was primarily centered around Gary Brooker's voice and piano, the guitar was often the main point of appeal, and on *Broken Barricades*, Robin's Stratocaster dominated all eight tracks. The album included three Trower compositions: "Memorial Drive," "Poor Mohammed," and his ode to Hendrix, "Song for a Dreamer." It was also his last album with the group, as a growing confidence in his own writing and playing prompted Trower to break away from the band at the height of its popularity.

"It was just a moment in time, I think, when I was ready to break out, and that was it," remembered Trower. "I gradually built up a lot of confidence on the road over in the States. Come the time of *Broken Barricades*, I had written some songs, but the thing that really did it was 'Song for a Dreamer.' I couldn't believe I did that."

Following his departure from Harum, Trower formed Jude, but the group soon disbanded, and Robin wasted no time in putting together his long-hoped-for trio, which features Jimmy Dewar on bass and vocals, and session man Reg Isidore on drums. The first album, entitled *Twice Removed from Yesterday*, embraces Robin's fluid Hendrixian style, as well as a musical freedom that was never before realized.

Robin readily admits the influence Hendrix had on him, and feels Jimi had as much impact on the guitar as Henry Ford did on the car. But in no way does he feel he is copying the late Stratocaster master. Rather, he defines his work as merely carrying on in Hendrix's path, and trying to recreate the aura that surrounded Jimi and his music.

In Procol Harum, Trower played a Gretsch Chet Atkins solidbody, two 1956 Les Pauls, and a Gibson SG Special. However, his last album with Harum showcased Robin on a Fender. But, oddly enough, Robin's switch to the Stratocaster wasn't prompted by Hendrix. During a tour with Jethro Tull, Robin arrived early for a soundcheck and found Martin Barre's Stratocaster (which Barre used for slide playing) propped up against an amplifier. Trower picked up the guitar, plugged it in, and with a shout that resounded around the auditorium yelled, "This is it!"

"I always felt there was something missing on Les Pauls," he said. "They had a good fat sound, but they never had that 'musical' sound. When I played a Strat I realized it had that strident chord. Also, the necks on Gibsons are too fat, and my fingers are a bit short. On Stratocasters, the neck is hardly there at all, and I like that very much."

Presently, he owns two Stratocasters, a black one that he deems unplayable, and a recently purchased white one that he feels is a real gem. Never altering his guitars, he has only two stipulations when it comes to buying one: It must be new, and it must have a maple neck. Maple necks, he explained, give a much "cleaner" sound than rosewood, although maple necks can be more difficult to play, in that the fretting hand tends to slip over the neck's smooth surface.

Robin strings his guitar with Ernie Ball strings, gauged .010, .012, .014, .020, .032, .042. His only real difficulty is in tuning the *D* string (because it's so light), but the overall sound he achieves with this combination far outweighs this minor problem. Robin doesn't find broken strings to be a dilemma, as he changes them every night after a show to ensure clear resonance during his next performance.

Pick choice is also important for Robin, because he has found that a light plectrum doesn't create any substantial sound at all, and one that is too heavy produces a wooden sound. His preference is an Ernie Ball Medium. Effects consist merely of a Univibe (heard prominently on his "Song for a Dreamer") and a custom volume booster (to deliver the extra punch needed when he solos).

Trower has established that Marshall is far and away the best amplifier for his needs. At the present time, he uses two Marshall 100-watt tops and two 4x12 cabinets for smaller halls, and adds two more 4x12s for larger auditoriums. The amps' gain stages are boosted at the Marshall factory in England to better produce the overdrive sound so reminiscent of Hendrix's playing. Trower sets the amp volume that around three-fourths full up, in order to achieve a nice flowing sound for chords, but not so loud that it will be unmanageable when he switches on the booster for a solo.

In the studio, Robin uses the same amplification setup that he utilizes on stage, but with the amps and guitar turned down to lower volumes. He finds that distortion does not sound as good recorded as it does live, so he tries to set the amplifiers as low as possible while still maintaining enough sustain.

Like Hendrix, Robin uses octaves considerably in his playing. Trower's runs are derived mainly from the blues scale, although he occasionally dips into a major scale (as in "Daydream") to produce a certain feeling.

"During the last year, I think I've progressed as far as sound, and getting much more out of the instrument," Robin said. "I mean, I'm beginning to understand it, although I'm not really conscious about anything I do. However, I like our things to be musical—I don't like just bludgeoning riffs. The electric guitar is the most expressive instrument—the nearest thing to the human voice, the human cry. The possibilities are limitless, really."

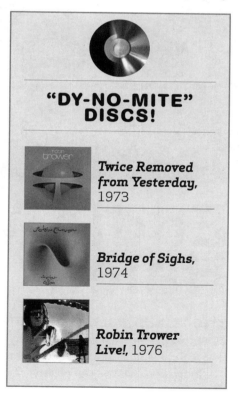

"DY-NO-MITE" DISCS!

Twice Removed from Yesterday, 1973

Bridge of Sighs, 1974

Robin Trower Live!, 1976

Eddie Van Halen shows how "air guitar" is *really* played.
(© TOLCA/SUNSHINE/RETNA LTD.)

Eddie Van Halen

ROCK AND ROLL IS FEELING. AND AFTER YOU KNOW most of the basics—chords, rhythm, scales, and bends—getting that feeling is just about the most important aspect of playing guitar.

In my opinion, you can't learn to play rock and roll by taking lessons.

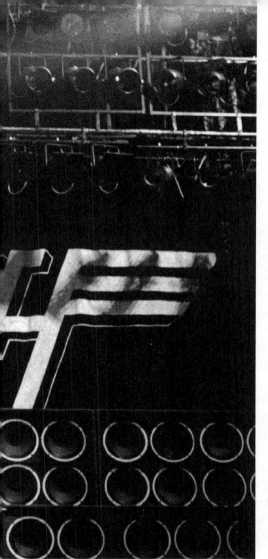

BY JIM FERGUSON

JULY 1984

Although a teacher can show you certain things—such as songs and licks—you still have to sit down and learn how things feel by listening. My biggest influence was Eric Clapton when he was with Cream and John Mayall's Bluesbreakers. I learned his solos to "Crossroads" [from Cream's *Wheels of Fire*], and "Sitting on Top of the World" [Cream, *Goodbye*] note for note by slowing them down to 16 RPM on my dad's phonograph. By taking licks off records and listening, I developed a feel for rock and roll. If you want to play, that's the same kind of thing you'll have to do. Eventually, you'll take the phrases and rhythm patterns you've copped and begin to put your own mark on them.

One of the areas that guys put too much emphasis on is equipment. Once, when Van Halen was on tour, we were opening for Ted Nugent, and he was standing there watching me play, wondering how I did it. The next day at the soundcheck, when I wasn't there, he asked our roadie if he could plug into my stuff. Of course, it still sounded like Ted. In other words, it doesn't really matter what you're playing through. Too many guys think a certain player's sound has to do with equipment, but it doesn't make any difference. Your sound is in your fingers and your brain.

If you're going to learn to play lead, get an electric guitar. It doesn't have to be an expensive one. I started on a cheapie Teisco Del Rey. Acoustic guitars aren't good for learning lead, because you can't play up very high on the neck, and they take heavier-gauge strings, which makes it hard to bend notes. I use light strings, Fender XLs. Also, you don't really need an amp at first, unless you're in a band. When I'm noodling around the house, I rarely plug in.

> 66 **When you finally master some of the basic ingredients of rock and roll, remember that your playing has to have feeling and taste.** 99

Most players want to learn lead because they think it's cool. Consequently, they never really develop good rhythm skills. But as most of a rock guitarist's time is spent playing rhythm, it's important to learn to do it well. Learning lead should come *after* you can play solid backup, and have the sound of the chords in your head. Playing blues progressions is the best place to start learning, because they're so basic, and they form the foundation for a lot of rock tunes. After you get one or two patterns down in a couple of keys, you can start noodling with lead guitar.

Before we talk further about playing lead, I want to touch on right-hand picking. Guys have pointed out that I hold my pick in two ways: with my thumb and middle finger, and with my thumb, index, and middle. Remember that most players don't pick the way I do, so what works for me might not work for you. The important thing about using the pick is that you alternate the picking direction: down, up, down, up, et cetera. This method really increases the efficiency of your picking hand. Once you get used to alternating strokes, you'll be able to pick without having to think about it.

The *A* pentatonic blues scale is the one most often used by blues and rock players. This scale fits many chords, including the entire 12-bar progression in *A*, and since it has five notes, it's called the pentatonic scale—*penta* is Latin for "five." If you already know this position, but still can't play lead very well, then you haven't worked with it enough. Once you learn some hammer-ons, pull-offs, slides, and bends, and how they're incorporated into licks, you'll see why the position is so common—and be sure to use alternate picking. Also, know the scale positions over the entire length of the fingerboard. Different positions can lend themselves to different licks, so once you have your scale patterns memorized, it's time to learn how to move them to other keys.

But knowing note locations is just the beginning. The next step is to start learning the building blocks of licks: hammer-ons, pull-offs, bends, and slides. Hammer-ons and pull-offs can give the notes you play fluidity and speed.

Bending is probably the technique most often associated with blues and rock soloing, and for that reason it's the most important one to learn. If you're a beginner, there are a couple of things to watch out for. First, don't overshoot the bend. By that, I mean don't bend a note beyond where you intend to go. And once a note is bent, be careful not to use too much finger vibrato—a singing effect produced by wiggling a string with a finger of your left hand right after it's been played. If your vibrato wavers too much, you'll overshoot the bend, and it'll sound weird. Lots of guys ask which notes I like to bend the most, and I always say, "All of them." And that's true—depending on the song I'm playing.

When you finally master some of the basic ingredients of rock and roll, remember that your playing has to have feeling and taste. The goal is to make music, not always to play machine gun–type stuff. To me, music is entertainment. You shouldn't be playing it to save the world, or show people how great you are. It's just supposed to make you happy, make you cry, make you get horny, or whatever. If it doesn't do that, then it's not music.

And remember: You learn by making mistakes. Don't be afraid to try something new. If I'm thrown into an unfamiliar situation—such as playing with Alan Holdsworth—I don't panic. Sometimes I skin my knees, but, most of the time, I land on my feet. My dad has a Dutch saying that puts it much better than I can. Translated, it means: "Ride your bicycle straight through." If you screw up, just keep going.

"DY-NO-MITE" DISCS!

Van Halen, **Van Halen,** 1978

Van Halen II, **Van Halen,** 1979

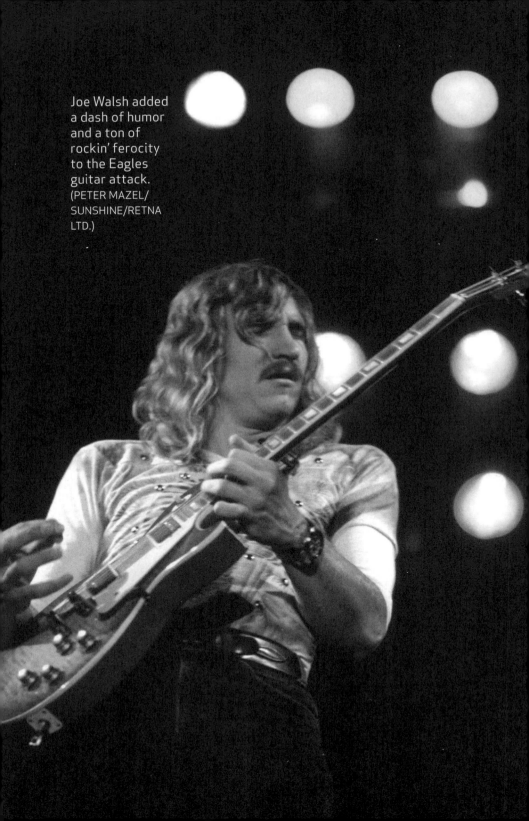

Joe Walsh added a dash of humor and a ton of rockin' ferocity to the Eagles guitar attack. (PETER MAZEL/ SUNSHINE/RETNA LTD.)

BY STEVE ROSEN

JUNE 1975

Joe Walsh

JOE WALSH PLAYS WITH THE GRACE OF GEORGE Harrison and the vehemence of Pete Townshend, a combination that earmarked his playing as lead guitarist of the James Gang. Raised in Ohio, he was weaned on the Beach Boys and the old rock and roll era (Elvis Presley, Chuck Berry), and grew up during the magical times of the Beatles and the *Sgt. Pepper* days. Quite oddly, Joe first began playing bass in high school (he attended Kent State also) because "it was easier—it only had four strings," and for the simple reason that the only "hot" band in town needed a bass player and not a guitarist. After this first experience with the Nomads, he soon developed an awareness of the actual structure of songs ("I listened to the radio four hours a day") and channeled his playing into a more technical arena.

It wasn't until Joe was in college that he seriously picked up a guitar. His stay at Kent State lasted three quarters, after which he became a part-time student and occupied himself with classes like electronics, music theory, and welding.

"I became the phantom of Kent State," he recalls, "taking all these weird courses that nobody could quite understand."

Though Walsh was versed on the six-string before his university days, after his first nonproductive year at Kent he was supporting himself with music. His first instrument was a Kay, which was pow-

ered by a little Fender amplifier with an eight-inch speaker that he says went "razzzzzzzz." While in college, he fluctuated between Fender and Gibson guitars, and when the Beatles grew to prominence, he went through a Vox amp and Rickenbacker guitar stage.

"The Rickenbackers were lousy guitars," Joe says, "but everybody had to have one because the Beatles used them."

Slowly, Joe started turning his attention to the new wave of British guitarists. Eric Clapton and Jeff Beck were two great influences on his playing, and it was listening to their records for hours each day that formed the basis of his style. In 1966, he was able to put his perpetual practice to use when he replaced Glen Schwartz as lead guitarist for the James Gang. At that point, he was using one of the newer model Gibson Flying Vs and a Fender amplifier. Realizing the potential opportunity to display all his months of solitary labors, he furthered his playing by bringing to the fore his college courses on electronics, wiring, soldering, and the like. What Joe refers to as "hotwiring" was an important part of his sound, and included the reworking of guitars and amps.

"I removed the tone condenser and capacitor in Telecasters," he explains, "so as to make the forward pickup hotter. I made the Telecaster pickups stronger by winding wire around the magnets, and I made them more sensitive by winding smaller wire—and consequently *more* of it—around the pickup. I also took the chrome covering off the humbucking pickups on Gibson guitars, and I put different tubes in amplifiers to make them louder."

He adds that even the basics are important in altering sound—how the neck is joined to the body, the bridge design, what type of strings, wood type of the guitar, and how the tone and volume circuits are wired.

"I'd experiment with stuff like that," Walsh says, "and I found that it not only changed the volume, but it also changed the sound. You put the pickup right up under the string, and it'll be louder. Just little things like that."

The guitarist recorded four albums with the Gang: *Yer Album*, *James Gang Rides Again*, *Thirds*, and *In Concert*. After that, Joe became tired and decided to stretch out on his own. Throughout, Joe has consistently demonstrated a penchant for a range of guitar sounds which, coupled with his chunky-rhythm funky lead style, are instantly discernible as his own.

"I like to switch guitars," he confirms, and consequently uses a two-year old Tele and a 1954 Stratocaster for recording, and a 1959 sunburst Les Paul for performing. On stage, Walsh amplifies his Paul with a beefed-up Fender Twin.

"Fender puts in little things to make it sound nice," he says, "and I took some things out to make it sound not nice. In the Fender tops with a bright switch, there is a yellow capacitor that goes between the bright switch and the treble control. By taking the capacitor off the normal channel and putting it in parallel with the vibrato channel, the result is a much boosted gain and, hence, greater highs. The capacitor is simply unsoldered from the normal side, and put in exactly the same position as the bright side capacitor. The wires are soldered in the same fashion as the part already there."

The reason for this setup—besides stronger highs—is to compensate for the loss of gain in an amp, which is first noticed in a decline in highs when longer guitar cords are used (especially when they are run through a wah-wah or Echoplex or some other auxiliary device).

Walsh uses a variety of appliances on stage, including a Leslie, a Fender echo, and a Maestro phase shifter. The echo employs a shielded cable, which is an inner conductor surrounded by wire to stop hum. Originally, the cable was in a footswitch, but Joe found that hooking it up to the phaser creates a brighter signal and greater phasing. Also, even when the echo unit is not switched on, he runs his signal through it because it adds a slight boost to the sound. A Vox wah-wah (and/or a Cry Baby) is also employed.

"It just depends on what sound I want at the moment," Walsh says. "I might run through a Leslie and an Echoplex, or a phaser and a Leslie. I might hook up something that sounds good, and then I'd hook it up again, and it wouldn't sound good. I like to keep changing."

During his constant metamorphosis, this inventive musician has stumbled upon other guitar and amplifier arrangements worth noting. One such reworking involves the Pignose amp. Besides the constant wearing out of batteries, the Pignose power supply is vastly insufficient when required to transmit strong signals. Joe explains how he solved the dilemma: "I secured a workbench power supply that includes a meter so as to adjust the voltage. Then, I cut the cables on the existing Pignose power unit and removed it. Next, you shear the two wires of the exterior plastic and attach the workbench unit. The new power source should be a nine-volt package. Heathkit makes an especially good one, and administers one to one-and-a-half amps of regulated power. The sound is no longer mushy, nor does it break up when the amp is turned full on."

Another device he came across—which is growing ever more popular—is the "talk box." Heard on his solo in "Rocky Mountain Way," this arrangement was first introduced to Joe by Bill West (husband of the country and western singer Dottie West).

"What is required for this process," Walsh says, "is the driver from a speaker. This is the unit screwed on the back of a speaker and can be found on the back of various amplifier speakers and on outdoor speakers such as those found around swimming pools and tennis courts. Dismantle the driver from the speaker—a 30-watt driver is more than satisfactory—and by either stapling, gluing, taping, or using epoxy, attach to the horn a plastic tube which can fit into your mouth.

"This entire assembly is then hooked up to the speaker jack, so—instead of a speaker—you have this cord going to a horn, a sound coming from it, and the signal finally emanating from the speaker itself. When you put the tube into the mouth, a process of modulation causes the distorted sounds to be heard. Do not talk into the tube—just move the mouth in simulation of talking, and allow the tube to act as the larynx. The signal is too weak to be used without amplification by means of a microphone or PA system. Also, before inserting the tube into your mouth, make sure that the grounds on the amplifier and driver unit are in synch."

Fender Rock and Roll strings are Walsh's choice—with the gauges ranging from .009 to .042—and he adjusts his strings close to the pickup to get more sustain ("For that Eric Clapton sound, you know?"). He feels that Fender strings last and don't break, and for slide he also chooses Fender, but the heaviest gauge. He uses both a glass and a metal slide, but—because his hands are so large—he cannot use the mini slides and small glass bottles used by other slide players.

"Duane Allman used to use a Coricidin bottle," Walsh points out, "but I can't use them because I can't get my finger in them."

E and *G* tunings are both used for slide, and Walsh uses Herco medium picks.

"I just go into a store," he says, "and see what they've got—whatever's around!"

For a while, he was experimenting with pedal-steel guitar after listening to Al Perkins. Other steel players Walsh likes are Sneaky Pete Kleinow, Rusty Young, and any other instrumentalist who can relate country to rock.

Joe occasionally dabbles in acoustic music, and, for this, he uses Gibson and Martin guitars.

"Ovations are eccch!" he exclaims. "I've never found a good neck yet, and they keep slipping off my lap."

Because of its superior sound, Joe says he would ultimately choose a Martin over a Gibson, though he dislikes the difficulty of repairing a damaged neck on a Martin, as its truss rod is nonadjustable except at the factory.

With regard to playing, Joe offers some ideas. He explains that, as all sound is a question of resonance, you may increase the sustain of notes by positioning yourself at various distances from the amplifier. Lower notes demand different distances than higher ones to resonate. Tunings are another way to expand one's playing, and oftentimes simply using a nonstandard tuning can take a player down an avenue he would not have ordinarily found. Also, the use of quarter notes (listen to the break in "Funk 49") can help add variety. After years of study, Joe has elevated himself to such a level that he says he no longer needs to capture every note on a Led Zeppelin or Cream album, or to listen to other guitarists for ideas. His technical skills have developed enough so that he is now able to express himself.

"Now, people are listening to me, so I just listen to myself play now," he says. "This is why new guitarists have to play their asses off, and play in front of people and experiment. Go back five years and listen to all those guitarists—the Yardbirds, James Burton with Ricky Nelson, Albert King—and learn all their licks, and find out where they learned them. You have to start at the beginning, get your left hand doing what your brain wants it to, and then, after a couple years, you'll get that. Once you get the technical end down, express yourself, and teach yourself. It's a long, hard trip, but if somebody starts, and does what I say, maybe in two or three years they'll play some hot licks. And I hope they do, because then *I* can copy them!"

"DY-NO-MITE" DISCS!

James Gang Rides Again, James Gang, 1970

Barnstorm, 1972

The Smoker You Drink, the Player You Get, 1973

Leslie West: — the Mountain man of heavy riffs. (COURTESY OF *GUITAR PLAYER* MAGAZINE)

BY FRED STUCKEY

APRIL 1972

Leslie West

THERE IS NO MISTAKING LESLIE WEST ON STAGE.
Hulking but easygoing, he is Mountain's dominant instrumental voice. His forcefully visceral guitar playing provides the counterpoint for leader Felix Pappalardi's schooled sophistication on the bass. Not a bad combination. As a booking agent in Los Angeles puts it: "Mountain is the first band in years that can get people off in the same magical way that Cream did."

Mountain has made the big time, so West can afford to relax a little by fooling around with his dog and four cats in the backyard of his country home in Woodstock, New York, or watching wrestling matches on TV with his wife in their London flat. But things haven't always been that easy.

West was born on October 22, 1945, in an Army hospital in Queens, New York. His father owned a rug-cleaning company, and Leslie lived comfortably until his parents were separated. He spent a lot of time in the streets, but he was sparked with ambition when he saw Elvis Presley's notorious appearance on *The Ed Sullivan Show* in the mid-1950s. He wanted to learn to play the guitar like Elvis, so his grandfather bought him an old tenor guitar in a pawnshop. He learned three chords and played

"Heartbreak Hotel" in a seventh-grade talent show. But that wasn't the beginning of a professional career.

"Playing three chords isn't really playing the guitar," says West.

After attending more than ten private schools, West discontinued his formal education at the end of the tenth grade. He tried making jewelry for a while, and worked at odd jobs. With the proceeds from his bar mitzvah, he was able to put together the money to buy an electric guitar, and not long afterwards, he saw the Beatles in New York on their first tour. This inspired him to form the Vagrants—his first professional undertaking. At that time, he was playing a scratched Telecaster. But along with his professional status, he wanted a shiny, new guitar, so he traded the Fender in on a Kent—a decision he has regretted ever since.

> **" You can feel as soon as you hit the note if it is going to go into that sustain. You can hold it for days if your guitar is wide open. "**

The Vagrants played the usual club tunes—like "Respect" and "In the Midnight Hour"—in the usual clubs. They filled out their gigs by working "sweet 16s"—private birthday parties given by parents in honor of their teenage daughters. The band was paid an average of $100 to perform at the parties, but "it came out to about $3 a man after we got finished paying for the dinner jackets and everything." During one stretch in a New York club, West and the Vagrants met the Rascals, who were playing a job down the street.

"We thought we were better than the Rascals until we saw them live," West remembers.

The Rascals introduced Leslie to an agent who helped the Vagrants put together two demo tapes, and, ultimately, negotiate a contract with Atlantic. Bassist and Cream producer Felix Pappalardi was called in to produce a single for the band. Later, West left the Vagrants and made arrangements for a solo album—titled *Mountain*—that Pappalardi also agreed to work on. Once the album was completed, Pappalardi left for England to produce a record with Cream bassist Jack Bruce. West decided that he wanted to get together more permanently with Pappalardi, with the result that Mountain (named after West's album) was formed in late 1969, when the bass player returned to New York.

"It wasn't until I saw Cream live that my head really got turned around," says West. "The Vagrants were into smashing their equipment and playing games and trying to act like the Who. Then, I saw Clapton, and that did it. I thought I'd better shit or get off the pot."

Unlike most rock guitar players who look for their roots in the blues, West was most influenced by Presley, Clapton, Keith Richards, and Pete Townshend (the Who is his all-time favorite band). He recognizes the importance of pop music and rock and roll in the formation of his own dynamic, hyper-amplified style. At a time when rock has turned in a mellow, lyrical direction, Mountain has kept the energy and drive of high volume, and merged it with the subtlety of classical and jazz motifs.

When touring with Mountain, West plays three guitars—a Les Paul Junior, a Flying V, and a Plexiglas Dan Armstrong. If the Les Paul Junior gets wet from perspiring hands during a set, he uses the Flying V for "Mississippi Queen," Mountain's encore number. He uses the Armstrong strictly for bottleneck. Because West liked the distortion provided by tube amplifiers, he used Marshall and Sunn amps early in his career.

"I was over in Germany doing this TV show, and this guy had some amps there," says West. "I tried them out, and gave him some advice about changing a few things like the speakers."

Those amps—the Stramp brand—will soon be available on the market as the Leslie West Professional Series. On stage and in the studio, he uses two stacks of Stramp amplifiers to get a sound that he thinks is similar to Marshall amp distortion. West claims that one of the advantages of the Stramp amplifier is that it is less prone to "blowing up" than the Marshall amplifier.

"Those Stramps feel like little bulldogs," he says.

The Stramp amplifiers have 100-watt brains and metal grilles to prevent the 12" Celestion speakers from being punctured. Interested musicians will ultimately be able to order Stramp amplifiers that will be exactly the same in all details as the ones used by West during live performances. Guitar players often order amps used by professionals because of the sound the professionals get with the equipment. What they don't realize, West says, is that the equipment has been modified, and they wind up with amplifiers from the factory that don't sound the same.

West rests the side of the palm of his right hand on the bridge of the guitar—or on the strings he is not picking—but his picking technique seldom allows his hand to remain in a stationary position for very long. Along with a pick, he occasionally uses his third finger for double picking, and says he wants to work on developing the use of his fourth finger to aid in multi-string picking.

"When I use a pick—and I use one most of the time—I try to bury it between my thumb and my first finger, and just let a little bit of the corner stick out," he explains. "I can easily get harmonics that way. Albert King does it without using a pick—he uses his thumb. It really is a great sound, because if I'm playing, say, on the *B* string, and all of a sudden I want a note that will really stick out and be an important part of the phrase, I can make a note jump an octave by hitting that harmonic."

A good example of West's harmonic technique is the last note of his solo in the middle section of "Theme for an Imaginary Western." He also uses the technique during the guitar solo of "Dream Sequence" [*Flowers of Evil*] to sustain a single note for a long period of time.

"The note catches, man," he says. "There is a feeling you get. You can feel as soon as you hit the note if it is going to go into that sustain. You can hold it for days if your guitar is wide open."

For Mountain's last album, *Flowers of Evil*, West used a hammering technique with his left hand that produces a violin-like sound. He hammers on a string with his guitar volume down, and then turns up the volume to get a whining sound. West hasn't used a fuzz tone in four years, and he gets vibrato strictly through the natural control of his fingers and wrist.

"Vibrato is all about control—it's like a voice, you know," he says. "Some opera singers control their voice to get that slow vibrato. Eric Clapton has about the best

"DY-NO-MITE" DISCS!

Nantucket Sleighride, Mountain, 1971

Flowers of Evil, Mountain, 1971

The Great Fatsby, 1975

vibrato I've ever heard in my life. Hendrix and Mick Taylor have beautiful vibratos, too. I'd take these guys over anybody else, because they control the whole thing. Some guitar players hit a note, and go into a vibrato that's really fast and intense with no control—which sounds like an opera singer with a bad voice."

Leslie uses La Bella and Darco strings—though one of Mountain's roadies actually puts them on the guitars. The top three strings are La Bella Extra Light, and the bottom three strings are Darcos, gauged .045, .035, and .028.

The chord structures and tempo changes of Mountain's music are sophisticated and demand high levels of musicianship, as shown in the recurrent theme that West plays in "King's Chorale." And he picks it all up by ear. When Pappalardi writes a tune that he wants West to learn, he makes up a simple, chord chart with the number of beats per chord. Within that context, West is free to devise his own phrasing.

"To tell you the truth, man, I don't know the names of the chords I play," he says. "I got the chord book that *Guitar Player* sent me, but it didn't do a bit of good. I can't read music. I can't even look at chord-position charts and play them. Instead, I would listen to records, or watch somebody fingering the guitar, and then I'd copy what they did by pretending I had a guitar in my hand. If you have a will, you can learn anything."

Johnny Winter rein-vigorated Muddy Waters's career when he produced the blues legend's *Hard Again* album in 1977. (COURTESY OF *GUITAR PLAYER* MAGAZINE)

BY DON MENN

AUGUST 1974

Johnny Winter

BEGINNING WITH HIS GREAT-GRANDMOTHER'S 100-year-old Spanish guitar with a neck "all horribly warped like a bow," Johnny Winter—the Texas blues rocker—has been stringing guitars since he was 11. He has worked his way through the years with first a Gibson ES-125, then a white Stratocaster, a couple of Gibson Les Paul Customs (one gold, one white), and a 1966 Fender Mustang.

With allowance money earned by mowing grass and lugging out garbage, Beaumont, Texas' best-known guitarist began accumulating his gigantic record collection of rock and roll (Carl Perkins, Elvis Presley, Little Richard, Fats Domino, et cetera), post-war Chicago blues (Muddy Waters, Howlin' Wolf, Otis Rush, Sonny Boy Williamson, et cetera), and, later, the blues of the Mississippi Delta, of Louisiana, and Texas.

"Lightnin' Slim and Lonesome Sundown and Lazy Lester—I mixed all that stuff up," Winter recalls. "A lot of it was still on 78s, but on the backs of albums by people like Muddy Waters, I'd read about Robert Johnson, Son House, Leadbelly, and Blind Lemon. When their albums finally did come out, I'd remember their names and buy them—buy the Delta blues."

When did you first get involved in music?

I started playing clarinet, but the orthodontist said I was going to have a bad overbite and that I'd better quit, so I found a ukulele around the house, and Daddy taught me a few chords. I had a rabbit that I liked a whole lot, and when the rabbit died, my great grandfather felt sorry for me, and bought me a baritone uke. I played that for a couple of years—me and [his brother] Edgar doing those barbershop-quartet harmony things that daddy would teach us, like "Ain't She Sweet" and "Bye Bye Blackbird." I didn't want

> 66 It really takes years if you're going to do it right. 99

to play guitar for a long time because my hands were too small, and those fingering positions were too strange. But daddy said, "The only two big ukulele guys I can think of are Ukulele Ike and Arthur Godfrey, so you don't really have too much chance playing ukulele. You'd better try guitar!" And when rock and roll started coming out, and there weren't any uke players in rock that I really liked, I thought, "Okay, I'll try guitar."

How did you first get acquainted with the blues?

There was this black disc jockey on this black station in Beaumont who was also a guitar player. His name was Clarence Garlow. He had a blues show, and I called him up and asked him to play songs on the air for me. We got to be friends, and I'd go down to his show. He's the first guy who really played the blues that I ever came into contact with. He played like a mixture of the blues and Cajun stuff like Clifton Chenier: French-oriented blues. He was a weird guy, but he was nice. Not too many white people were into blues, and Clarence could tell I was really digging it, so he didn't mind taking the time out. It was like I was his protégé. I'd come down and he'd show me things. He'd play anything I wanted to hear.

He was the first guy who turned me on to unwound thirds [strings]. I'd listen to those blues records like Bobby Bland and Otis Rush, and I wondered, "How can they bend their strings like that?" I mean, I was using a regular old set of Gibson Sonomatics [laughs]! So I used a whole lot of the tremolo bar, and I got that down until it sounded pretty close to where it should. Then, I found what most people did was to take a second string and use it for the third, and they'd play with the regular bottom strings, two second strings, and then a first. And then I wanted to get real cool. I used a second string for the third, a first string for the second, and an *A*-tenor banjo string for the first. That was really cool—a really hot lick! To say the least, it helped a lot.

Was Clarence Garlow your only teacher?

No, there were several guys. I never took lessons to learn how to read music, or where to put my fingers. I would just ask these guys to show me whatever they thought I ought to know. The guy that really started me off was Luther Nallie—a really good country guitar player. The last time I talked to him he was playing bass with Roy Rogers [*laughs*]. Luther was working at Jefferson Music Company in Beaumont. I guess he thought I was good, and we got to be really good friends. I really dug fingerstyle—Merle Travis/Chet Atkins things. I still love those guys. Country and western was all around, and Luther played real good country and western. He'd show me things like "Honky Tonk." He'd really go to a lot of trouble. If I'd ask him to show something to me he didn't know, he'd go and get the record, figure it out, and come back and show me. When I got interested in blues, Luther really didn't know too much at all about that, but I knew enough to go on from there by myself by listening to records and learning the licks.

When you were learning from records, did you steal licks, or did you just get the feel?

I would just learn how to play a record note for note. After I kind of got the feel of what was supposed to be going on, I just took what I heard and assimilated it, and I guess it would come out part mine and part everybody else's. There's nobody that really plays original. You can't. You can find some of everybody's licks in almost everybody's playing, but I tried to make it my own after I got the basic things down.

When you started playing blues, where did you perform?

I'd go to black clubs. I'd get a few gigs, and I'd go sit in at places like the Raven. I met B. B. King there when I was about 18, and I jammed with him. We were the only white people in a club of about 1,500 people. Nobody bothered us at all. Everybody was real cool, because I knew them from hanging around there. So B. B. was playing, and I wanted to show off so bad, man. I wanted him to know I could play, and the more I drank, the more I wanted to sit in. Then, a few of my black friends came over and said, "Come on, man, why don't you sit in with B. B.?" So finally I went up and asked him if I could. B. B.

234 GUITAR PLAYER PRESENTS GUITAR HEROES OF THE '70S

thought I was crazy. He said, "Can I see a union card?" I whipped out my union card, and that shook him up, because that usually gets them, you know. I mean, if I were him, I wouldn't let anybody play. It was absurd, man. Some little white kid asking to sit in and play. He said, "Well, you don't know our songs." I said, "Man, I know your songs. I know *all* your songs." "Let me think about it," he said.

So then my friends come over and said, "Is he going to let you?"

"I don't know," I said. "Why don't you go ask him?"

Finally, about 300 black people started yelling, "Come on—let him sit in, man." B. B. realized that even if I wasn't any good, I had enough friends there that it wouldn't hurt to let me make an ass out of myself, so he let me play. I did one of his tunes, and everybody just flipped out. This was before any white people wanted to be a part of that scene, and those people knew I was really sincere, and that I loved their music.

B. B. told me, "Man, you're great. Keep on doing it, and you'll be successful someday."

I saw him again years later, and he remembered me immediately. He hugged me, and said all kinds of great things about me in all of his interviews. He really helped me a lot. I kept hanging out at the Raven and jamming with whoever I could until the race thing started getting weird. A lot of younger black people were starting to resent white people coming into their club, so I didn't feel comfortable and I quit hanging out there. It was a mixture of things. It was partly, "You haven't let us in your clubs, so why should we let you in our clubs?" And it was also because, by that time, the blues got to be a thing they didn't like. They didn't want black people playing it, much less white people. The blues was a disgrace to them—it was the music of poor, ignorant black people. Before, you'd go to somebody's house, and you'd see Lightnin' Hopkins and Muddy Waters records, but, after a while, they'd break those records and get the Nina Simone albums. The blues just went out. The black people were ashamed of it, and white people didn't like it yet. So there was just nobody to hear it until the young English guys started picking up on it.

What sort of guitars are you using now?

Gibson Firebirds. I love Firebirds.

Where do you set the tone and volume controls?

Everything on all the way.

And what about your amps?

I'm using a Marshall 100-watt stack. Everything up all the way, except no bass.

What are using for a slide?

I was using test tubes, playing with the back of my wristwatch—everything imaginable. Then, a friend of mine in the Denver Folklore Society said I'd better go to a plumbing supply place, get a 12-foot long piece of conduit pipe, and have it cut into pieces and rounded on one side. When I got it, it was kind of a dull gray, and real rough. Then, I just played and wore that off, and it became kind of a shiny black. I played it for a little while longer, and wore that off, and now it's kind of silver. Crust just sort of built up inside—rust and dirt and sweat and everything. I love it! I don't even have any backup slides. I don't know how I've managed to keep myself together enough to keep this slide for five years [*laughs*]. I started out putting the slide on my ring finger, until my friend advised me to switch to my little finger so I could play chords.

What sort of strings are you using?

The gauges are .009, .011, .016, .024, .032, .042—the brand doesn't matter. I change them when they break [*laughs*].

Do you use any tone modifying devices?

No. That stuff is so complicated that it just freaks me out. When I try any kind of gadget, it ends up ruining the show. A gadget will work just fine in practice, but as soon as I use it in concert, it gets stage fright and freaks out. So I decided that stuff wasn't right for me.

What tunings are you using?

Open *A* and open *E*. Sometimes, I play slide in regular tuning, but not too often.

You once said that you and Jimi Hendrix didn't jam well together because you respected each other too much.

Yeah, we'd both just lay back and wait for the other one. I loved his stuff, and I felt weird with him playing rhythm. I'd

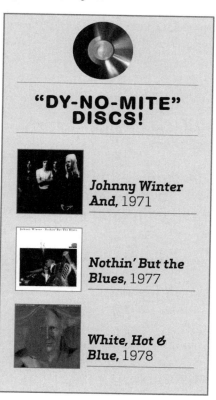

"DY-NO-MITE" DISCS!

Johnny Winter And, 1971

Nothin' But the Blues, 1977

White, Hot & Blue, 1978

play a little bit, and then I'd lay back and wait for him to play. Then, he'd start laying back and waiting for me to play.

Do you have any advice for upcoming musicians?

In the early days, nobody had the technical ability that they do nowadays. There weren't really good, fancy, rock and roll guitar players. Chuck Berry was the best, but it was pretty much just rhythmic things, and it was a struggle for guitar players to just play Chuck Berry stuff. He was like the Jimi Hendrix of the '50s.

Now, kids are coming up with a lot more technical ability, but they don't know exactly how to use it—how to fit it in with taste. You can't just throw in things, and say, "Look, man, I can play a bunch of notes. I can play as fast as Alvin Lee!" Some people will put stuff like that in some song where it doesn't have the least bearing on anything else that's going on. I guess things are so speeded up now that the general attitude is, "I want it, and I want it now." A lot of kids just don't want to take the time to work on it—see where it's all going, what it means, where it comes from, and how they should apply it and use it in playing their songs. It really takes years if you're going to do it right.

Ron Wood—wielding a Zemaitis guitar—often "weaves" his Stones' licks into Keith Richards's parts.
(ROBERT MATHEAU/RETNA LTD.)

BY STEVE ROSEN

DECEMBER 1975

Ron Wood

DURING THE MUSICALLY BOUNTIFUL YEARS
of the late '60s, the Jeff Beck Group emerged. It was
an outfit of undisciplined nature and unabashed energy.
Featuring Beck on guitar and Rod Stewart on vocals, the
band focused primarily on these two members, but
below the flash was the lifeblood of the quintet. Bassist
Ron Wood laid down flowing lines, around which Jeff
and keyboardist Nicky Hopkins improvised; and it was
Wood's ingenious fretwork which helped to make the
band's first album, *Truth*, a (now-realized) rock classic.
This early association with Stewart led to Ron's more
recent position as lead guitarist with the Faces, and asso-
ciations with the English rock scene in general most
recently led to his enrollment as second guitarist with
the Rolling Stones on their 1975 tour.

Wood first began playing guitar when he was eight,
on a loaned instrument from a friend who was joining
the army. He used the guitar for two years, until his com-
panion returned from service and
resumed ownership. For nearly two
years after that, Ron was without an
instrument, until his brother's
friends chipped in to buy him a guitar
that cost five pounds (£12).

"It had really quite bad action on
it," Wood recalls. "It was only an old

beat-up acoustic. But I would often play in my bedroom. There was a little record player with a tiny little speaker, and I just used to learn solos by ear."

Ron's biggest influence in those early years was Chuck Berry, so it was not too surprising when a few years later, at age 14, he purchased an electric. Costing $60, it came from the local record shop and served as his first serious experience in music. He also acquired a Bird amplifier, which provided the only amplification for several amateur groups he was involved with.

> **❝ I'd heard Duane Allman on record, I didn't know who was playing, but I just thought, 'That sounds great—that's the only direction to go in.' ❞**

"The vocals, two guitars, and bass went through the Bird," Ron says. "I was the lead guitarist. I had that title."

Born near the London Airport in the Middlesex area, Ron was weaned on the early Motown scene. Marvin Gaye and Eddie Hollander are a couple of the artists whose music he played. That early group was called the Thunderbirds (eventually evolving into the Birds, not to be confused with the Byrds), and as primitive as the music was, Ron feels the people listening were even more so.

"That was the time," he states, "when people thought there were special guitars for rhythm and lead."

Wood reached a saturation point with the Birds, and—not quite knowing what he was looking for—he left the band.

That search ended when Ron met with Jeff Beck, who had just left the Yardbirds and was giving thought to forming his own group. The two musicians had a working relationship of sorts, since the Birds (playing six nights a week up and down the English countryside) often backed the Yardbirds.

"I suppose Jeff was one of my best friends," Wood states, "even though he was in another band. When he left the Yardbirds, my group had already wilted and was just about to fold, so that's when we got together."

This was in early 1967, and though Wood knew Beck, he was not too familiar with his playing. The only time he had really had a chance to see Jeff perform was when the guitarist was in a pre-Yardbirds band called the Tridents, and they used to support the Birds.

Unknown to many people is the fact that Wood first joined the Beck ranks as guitarist, and for several gigs the lineup read Wood and Beck on guitars, Dave Ambrose (then playing with Brian Auger) on bass, Rod Stewart on vocals, and Ray Cook on drums. This order was short-lived, due to creative emptiness, although when John Lord (organist for Deep Purple) saw this band perform he thought it was magic.

"He came to one show at the Marquee and thought it sounded great," Wood says. "He thought that it sounded best when it had two guitars."

Wood, however, didn't feel entirely comfortable playing guitar in a band with Jeff Beck, and was much more at ease allowing the established guitarist to handle all six-string duties. Following that first membership, Aynsley Dunbar came in on drums, and Ron remembers with particular satisfaction his role as one-half of that rhythm section. While Wood was on guitar, the band was playing much of the material that later showed up on *Truth*.

Ron really never asked Jeff for any guitar pointers, but the two often sat down together, and Beck would ask if Wood had ever tried this or that lick.

"We had a nice feel between us," Wood states, adding, "There was never any competition. I used to respect his playing, and I still do."

It was natural for Wood to come into the group as a guitarist since his previous training was on that instrument. The switch finally came after several rehearsals when Ambrose did not show up, and Jeff was in a quandary about who would play bass for the practice session. Ron offered his services, and after

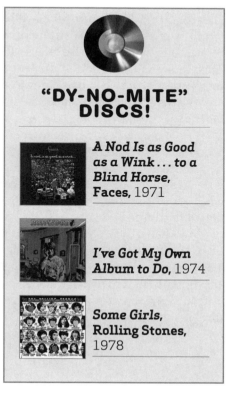

"DY-NO-MITE" DISCS!

A Nod Is as Good as a Wink . . . to a Blind Horse, **Faces,** 1971

I've Got My Own Album to Do, 1974

Some Girls, **Rolling Stones,** 1978

frequent switches to the bass, Beck asked if he wouldn't mind playing four-string permanently. Wood's first bass was a Fender Jazz he "obtained" from Sound City, a music store around the block from where they rehearsed.

"I had no money," he explains. "I couldn't pay for it, so I borrowed it and never took it back. About five years later, I paid for it—after they tracked me down."

Wood found it easy to play bass behind Beck, whose stylistic approach left a lot of holes, and it was up to Ron to fill them. He played a bass solo every night, and recently, when he heard a tape of the Beck band and his solo, he admitted, "They used to get good! I was knocked out, I wasn't so bad after all."

During the Beck days, Wood used a pick, as well as wire-wound strings. He played with a lot of treble on the guitar and amplifier. He was on bass for nearly four-and-a-half years and during that period never once lifted a six-string.

After the Beck outfit splintered (due to management and personality conflicts), Ron returned to a Gibson SG that he had prior to moving to bass guitar. That instrument was stolen and replaced by a red Stratocaster, which was also stolen, and in its place came a Danelectro. This, too, was taken, and in the end Wood resorted to having his guitars made. He learned about Tony Zemaitis and approached him.

"No one would dare steal his guitars because he makes them so individual," Ron says. "He plasters your name all over it."

The move back to guitar was, quite oddly, a "natural" process for Wood, and his feel for the instrument had so expanded that the first thing he practiced was bottleneck guitar—a style he had never attempted.

"I'd heard Duane Allman on record," he explains. "I didn't know who was playing, but I just thought, 'That sounds great—that's the only direction to go in.'"

Wood now incorporates a lot of slide work in his playing, using an open-E tuning on one guitar, with the others tuned normally. He uses a 3/4" copper pipe and states a liking for such players as Hound Dog Taylor, Earl Hooker (when he was with Muddy Waters and doing the original versions of songs like "You Shook Me" and "Little Brown Bird"), and Allman.

"But I only used these people as a starting block," he asserts. "I've gone my own sweet way since then."

Frank Zappa considered his guitar solos to be "compositions." (JORGEN ANGEL/RETNA LTD.)

Frank Zappa

FRANK ZAPPA—GUITARIST, COMPOSER, PRODUCER, AVID roller-derby fan, and leader of the Mothers of Invention—is, at 36, probably the elder statesman of progressive rock and roll. In addition to leading his ever-changing, ever-expanding Mothers—which

BY STEVE ROSEN

JANUARY 1977

has included such notables as French jazz violinist Jean-Luc Ponty, keyboardist George Duke, drummer Aynsley Dunbar, and Mark Volman and Howard Kaylan (presently known as Flo and Eddie)—Zappa has continually served as one of the most articulate and controversial satirists on "pop-music weirdness."

Here is the unexpurgated story of Frank Zappa—his early influences, his guitar technique, his equipment changes through the years, and his approach to producing his own sound on record.

When did you start playing guitar?

I began when I was 18, but I started on drums when I was 12. I didn't hear any guitarists until I was about 15 or so, because in those days, the saxophone was the instrument that was happening on record. When you heard a guitar player, it was always a treat, so I went out collecting R&B guitar records. The solos were never long enough—they only gave them one chorus—and I figured the only way I was going to get to hear enough of what I wanted to hear was to get an instrument and play it myself. So I got one for a $1.50 in an auction—an archtop, f-hole, unknown-brand thing with the whole finish sanded off. The strings were about, oh, a good inch off the fingerboard [*laughs*], and I

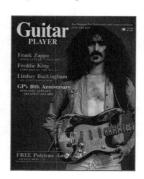

didn't know any chords, but I started playing lines right away. Then, I started figuring out chords, and I finally got a Mickey Baker book, and learned a bunch of chords from it.

Who were some of your early guitar influences?

I used to like Johnny "Guitar" Watson, Clarence "Gatemouth" Brown, Guitar Slim, and Matt Murphy.

When did you buy your first electric guitar?

I didn't get my first one until I was 21, when I rented a Telecaster from a music store. Then, I bought a Fender Jazzmaster—which I used for about a year and a half. I used to play, like, lounge jobs. You know, sit on the stool, strum four chords to a bar, "Anniversary Waltz," happy birthday, one twist number per night, and don't turn it up. Nobody else in the band really knew what the chord changes were to these dumb songs—they were all trying to figure out what was going on. I played places like Tommy Sandy's Club Sahara in San Bernardino, and some clubs around West Covina—really boring, miserable places. I worked with a group called Joe Perrino and the Mellowtones. Then, I got a chance to write some music for a western starring Mercedes McCambridge entitled *Run Home Slow* that was written by my English teacher. I actually earned something doing that film, so I used the money to buy a Gibson ES-5 Switchmaster. I recorded the first three albums with that guitar.

Besides the Switchmaster, what equipment did you use on *Freak Out!*?

Just a Fender Deluxe amp—that's all. After the Switchmaster, I got a goldtop Gibson Les Paul, and I used that for a couple of albums. Eventually, I got a Gibson SG.

Are you still using the SG?

I'm using a variety of things now. I've branched out quite a bit in the last couple of years. I have a couple of Stratocasters wired up in funny ways. Both have preamps built into them, and one has a special tone-control switch that lets you put each of the pickups out of phase. The other Strat has a Barcus-Berry pickup placed in the neck, which gives it a really interesting sound, because I do a lot of stuff with my left hand, and it helps the notes speak a lot faster. You can touch it any-place, and hear where you touch the guitar, because the Barcus-Berry hears everything. It's like the whole guitar is alive.

What specifically do you do with your left hand?

If I pick one note with my right hand, I'm playing five with my left.

I don't pick everything that I play, and, consequently, the action is kept pretty low on most of the guitars. I also do some stuff where I use the pick on the fingerboard, pressing down and hitting the string at the same time. It gets kind of a Bulgarian bagpipe sound. An example of that is on the end of the solo in "Inca Roads," and also on "Po-Jama People" [both from *One Size Fits All*].

As you've used both Fender and Gibson guitars, do you have any preference for one over the other?

I use them for the things they're good for. The Strat has a drier sound—more of an acute, exact sound—and Gibsons have more of a sweat-hog type of sound.

What type of wah-wah do you use?

I have a Mu-Tron, which I use as a tone control. Very seldom do I just step on it on the beat—like on the old Clapton records where he goes *wacka-wacka-wacka*. Usually, what I do is shape the notes for phrasing with it, and the motion of the wah pedal itself is very slight. I try to find one center notch in the thing that's going to emphasize certain harmonics, and ride it right in that area. If you put the pedal all the way down the tone is too squeaky, and if you put it all the way up it's too blurred.

What kind of picks and strings do you use?

I use Fender Heavy picks. As for strings, I use a different set for each guitar—mainly Ernie Balls—and I have about 22 guitars. To give you an idea, I use either an .008 or .009 for the high E, an .011 or .012 for the B, a .016 or .017 for the G, a .024 for the D, anywhere from .032 to .038 for the A, and anywhere from a .046 to a .052 for the low E.

What is your amp setup?

I use a 100-watt Marshall and an Acoustic 270 going into either a Vox 4x12 cabinet loaded with JBLs, or a Marshall 4x12 with JBLs.

Are there certain settings you use on the 270s equalizer to achieve certain sounds?

It depends on what kind of hall I'm playing in. I'm real fussy about equalization, and sometimes, there's a compromise between the kind of sound I want to get onstage, and what the mixer needs to hear out in the audience. I'll change things around for that.

I've used the 100-watt Marshall with the volume at about four. I double the inputs into the bass channel (with a connecting cord), and set the treble control to about four, and the bass to around three. Midrange is anywhere from six to eight, and presence will vary from six to ten. This is the average—the bass could be as high as ten, or as low as zero—depending on how much bottom is needed.

On the 270, the volume will be at four, the bright switch is on, treble is all the way up, midrange is at about 75 percent, and bass will be about 80 percent. The onboard graphic equalizer is all the way up at 80Hz, about 80 percent at 160Hz, all the way up at 320Hz, just about flat at 640Hz, and maybe a little bit of a boost at 1250Hz.

Is this the same setup you use when recording?

No. In the studio, most of the stuff is played through a tiny Pignose amp. I've done all kinds of things with a Pignose. I've put it in a live chamber, and stuck an Electro-Voice RE-20 microphone right in front of it. You can hear that the amp is in a room, and that the room is resonant—it's a realistic sound. Or I'll put it in an echo chamber, and move the mic back a bit to get even more resonance. The Pignose isn't real loud, so if you put the mic about a foot away from the amp, you get a sound that approaches what you'd hear in a hockey rink. Another thing I've done with the Pignose is to put it out in the middle of a dead studio, and then position two mics around it to get a good stereo sound. I'll sometimes put one mic behind the other to get a slight spread to the sound. I've been using a Pignose for about the last three or four years. I think I started using it the most on *Apostrophe*, but there is some on *Over-Nite Sensation*, too.

Are your solos on record improvised first takes, or are they conceived beforehand?

It depends on what the song is. Very rarely are they first-take things. But they also aren't things where I'd sit down and work out the whole solo in advance before I played it. I can't do that. I wouldn't remember it. Usually, what I do if I get something going, is that I'll lay down 20 bars or so, then stop the tape, back it up, punch in, and take up where I left off. I try to have the event that's going on the record make musical sense, and fit in with what's going on. This is because a record is a fixed object—it doesn't change. It's not a song anymore. It's an object. If you're playing a song on the road, it can change every night. It comes alive each time you play it. It has its own existence. But once you've committed a song to wax, it never changes. So if you're going to leave your guitar solo on, you're stuck with that for the life of the record. I'm fairly fussy about it, but I'm sure I let a few go out on record that I could probably do better now. But I hope that's the way it's always going to be.

What scales do you work from?

My solos are speech-influenced rhythmically. Harmonically, they're either pentatonic, or poly-scale oriented, and I also use the Mixolydian mode a lot.

You don't really play a lot of blues licks in your solos.

I can. I have. I started off that way. But I'm more interested in melodic things. I think the biggest challenge when you go to play a solo is trying to invent a melody on the spot. I also think that a guitar player can only be as good as the band that's accompanying him. If the people backing you up are sensitive to what you're playing, you'll sound great. If they're just note-mashers, then you'll always sound mundane.

What are the qualities you look for in a backing musician?

I've always had good rhythm-section players, but I wouldn't say they've always been too enthusiastic about what I was playing, or understood it very well, or really got into it. Because if a person is from the jazz world, they're going to play worlds of gnat notes that really don't amount to shit. Or if they're from the blues world, they want somebody who gets on three notes and goes "squirm-squirm-squirm." It's hard to explain to guys just coming into the band, the rhythmic concept I have about playing, because it's based on ideas of metrical balance— long, sustained events versus groupettoes that are happening with a lot of notes on one beat. A lot of sextuplets, septuplets—things like that. A lot of times, I'll play 13 notes over a half note, and try to space it evenly so it flows. This is sort of against the grain of rock and roll, which likes to have everything in exactly duple or triple, straight up and down, so you can constantly tap your

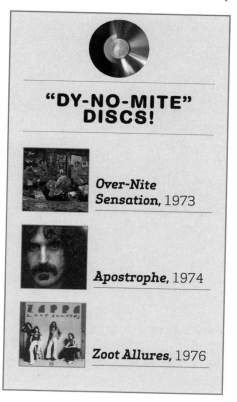

"DY-NO-MITE" DISCS!

Over-Nite Sensation, 1973

Apostrophe, 1974

Zoot Allures, 1976

foot to it. But I prefer to have the rhythm section be aware of where the basic pulse of the time is, and create a foundation that won't move, so I can flow over the top of it. It's hard to get people to do that, and it's also hard to get them to leave some space for where the fast notes occur. Rhythm sections always have a tendency to copy. If they hear somebody else playing fast notes, they want to play fast notes, too, and then you can't hear any fast notes any more.

How do you see your role as a guitarist different from players such Jeff Beck or John McLaughlin?

I think that's a matter of advertising more than anything else. Once I get onstage and turn my guitar on, it's a special thing to me. I love doing it. But I approach it more as a composer who happens to be able to operate an instrument called a guitar, rather than "Frank Zappa, Rock and Roll Guitar Hero."